Growing Together in Unity and Mission

Building on 40 years of Anglican – Roman Catholic Dialogue

An Agreed Statement of the
International Anglican – Roman Catholic
Commission for Unity and Mission

First published in Great Britain in 2007

Society for Promoting Christian Knowledge
36 Causton Street
London SW1P 4ST

British Library Cataloguing-in-Publication Data
A catalogue record for this book is available from the British Library.

ISBN 978-0-281-05939-3

10 9 8 7 6 5 4 3 2

Designed and typeset by Kenneth Burnley, Wirral, Cheshire
Printed in Great Britain by Ashford Colour Press

Produced on paper from sustainable forests

Preface

In May 2000 the Archbishop of Canterbury, Dr George Carey, and the President of the Pontifical Council for Promoting Christian Unity, Cardinal Edward Cassidy, called a meeting of bishops from our two Communions at Mississauga in Canada to seek a way forward in the continuing relationship between the Anglican Communion and the Catholic Church.

It was a meeting filled with hope for the future relationship between the two Communions, marked by a recognition of how much we shared in common in our Christian belief and ecclesial life.

At the end of our meeting, the bishops accepted that a new body should be established to promote our relationship by seeking to translate our manifest agreement in faith into common life and mission. This commission would be quite different from the existing theological dialogue of the Anglican – Roman Catholic International Commission (ARCIC). It was envisaged as a commission of bishops which would focus on the agreements discerned by ARCIC precisely to draw out how they compel us towards joint witness and mission in the world.

The International Anglican – Roman Catholic Commission for Unity and Mission (IARCCUM) was established in 2001 and its work since then has been to implement the mission plan agreed in Mississauga. The force of events, particularly difficulties in the life of the Anglican Communion, had its impact on the work of the Commission: some of these are detailed in paragraph 6.

This is not an authoritative declaration by the Roman Catholic Church or by the Anglican Communion. What is offered by IARCCUM here is a statement which is intended to foster discussion and reflection. However, it is more than this: it is a call for action, based upon "an honest appraisal of what has been achieved in our dialogue". Despite our present 'imperfect communion', there is, we feel, enough common ground to take seriously how we work together. IARCCUM, as an episcopal commission, is offering practical suggestions on the way in which Anglican and Roman Catholic ecumenical participation can be appropriately fostered and carried forward. Although this text has been prepared by bishops and is addressed primarily to bishops, it is to be hoped that bishops will in turn engage clergy and laity in responding to the challenges set out in the text, in ways appropriate to their local circumstances.

It is forty years since Archbishop Michael Ramsey paid the first formal visit of an Archbishop of Canterbury to the Pope, in this case Pope Paul VI, since the Reformation. Behind the divisions of the Reformation lay fifteen hundred years of communion in faith and witness. The time is ripe for reflection, which leads to intensified action. As co-chairs of IARCCUM we commend this document for joint study and action, and ask that God's Holy Spirit may continue to move us ever closer to that unity for which Christ prayed and for which Anglicans and Catholics yearn.

+ John Bathersby
Archbishop of Brisbane, Roman Catholic Co-Chair

+ David Beetge
Bishop of the Highveld, Anglican Co-Chair

Feast of Saint Francis, 4 October 2006

Part One

The Achievements of the Anglican – Roman Catholic Theological Dialogue

Introduction:
Commitment to unity and mission

1. Anglicans and Roman Catholics[1] agree that God desires the visible unity of all Christian people and that such unity is itself part of our witness. Our churches share a commitment to work for that unity in truth for which Christ prayed (John 17). We have each expressed this in our own internal statements and, since 1966, Popes and Archbishops of Canterbury have re-affirmed this goal of the restoration of visible unity and full ecclesial communion in their Common Declarations.[2]

2. It was with this end in mind that in 1966 Pope Paul VI and Archbishop Michael Ramsey called for the setting up of a theological dialogue. Since then, the Anglican – Roman Catholic International Commission (ARCIC) has produced a series of agreed statements addressing issues on which agreement is required if the two Communions are to live in visible unity. The first series of statements, published together under the title *The Final Report*, covered the areas of Eucharist, ministry and ordination, and authority.[3] *The Final Report* was presented to the authorities of both Communions and received official response. The Anglican Communion recognised the Eucharist and ministry statements as "consonant in substance with the faith of Anglicans".[4] An initial Roman Catholic response

---

1   In this document we have tried to use those terms most commonly used by churches to describe themselves, but sometimes context has meant that it has been preferable for the sake of clarity to refer to the 'Roman Catholic Church'. In using a variety of names, no theological position is being adopted intentionally by IARCCUM, which has sought to be fair to the self-understanding of both dialogue partners.

2   See Appendix I.

3   *The Final Report* (London: CTS/SPCK, 1982) included the statements *Eucharistic Doctrine* (1971); *Ministry and Ordination* (1973); *Authority in the Church I* (1976); an Elucidation of each of these three texts (*Eucharist* and *Ministry Elucidations* dated 1979, *Authority in the Church I Elucidation* dated 1981); and *Authority in the Church II* (1981). For a full listing of ARCIC documents, see Appendix II.

4   Resolution 8, Lambeth Conference of 1988.

requested further work in these two areas.[5] Clarifications prepared by an ARCIC sub-commission were subsequently judged by the Roman Catholic Church to have greatly strengthened agreement in these areas.[6] Both Communions recognised convergence in the area of authority, while acknowledging, as ARCIC itself had done, that significant issues remained to be addressed.[7] The second phase of ARCIC continued the search for further agreement in faith, addressing salvation and justification, ecclesiology, morals, authority and the place of Mary in the life of the Church. These documents have not yet received an official evaluation from the churches.[8] Through this theological dialogue over forty years Anglicans and Roman Catholics have grown closer together and have come to see that what they hold in common is far greater than those things in which they differ.

3.   Hand in hand with the work of theological dialogue, relationships have been developing between Anglicans and Roman Catholics in a variety of ways. As Archbishop George Carey and Pope John Paul II noted, "in many parts of the world, Anglicans and Catholics, joined in one baptism, recognise one another as brothers and sisters in Christ and give

---

5   'Catholic Response to the Final Report of ARCIC-I', initially published in *L'Osservatore Romano*, December 6, 1991; reprinted in *Information Service* 82 (1993/I), pp. 47–51.

6   'Clarifications of Certain Aspects of the Agreed Statements on Eucharist and Ministry', *Information Service* 87 (1994/IV), pp. 239–242. In his letter to the Co-Chairmen of ARCIC on March 11, 1994, Cardinal Edward Cassidy noted that the Clarifications had been "examined by the appropriate dicasteries of the Holy See" and that with regard to Eucharist and Ministry, "no further study would seem to be required at this stage" (*Information Service* 87 [1994/IV], p. 237). No formal Anglican response to Clarifications has been initiated.

7   Cf. Resolution 8, Lambeth Conference of 1988; 'Catholic Response to the Final Report of ARCIC-I'.

8   *Salvation in the Church* was welcomed as a "timely and significant contribution" by the Lambeth Conference in 1988, and commended for study across the Anglican Communion. The Congregation for the Doctrine of the Faith also offered observations on *Salvation in the Church* (London: CTS, 1989), noting that their judgement was "substantially positive" but not yet "able to ratify the final affirmation (no.32) according to which the Catholic Church and the Anglican Communion 'are agreed on the essential aspects of the doctrine of salvation and on the Church's role within it'".

expression to this through joint prayer, common action, and joint witness".[9] In diverse contexts, Anglicans and Catholics attempt to witness together in the face of rapid change, globalisation and fragmentation, growing secularism, religious apathy and moral confusion. In places, Anglican and Roman Catholic bishops meet regularly for consultation and prayer. Representatives of each tradition are invited to be observers at the conciliar gatherings of the other. Since the Second Vatican Council, Archbishops of Canterbury and Popes have met together on frequent occasions, praying together for the Church and for the world. Their joint declarations affirm the degree of communion that is already shared, as well as the urgency of continuing together on the way to visible unity.

A further step

4.   In May of 2000, building on the reflections of Pope John Paul II and Archbishop George Carey in their Common Declaration of 1996, a meeting of Anglican and Roman Catholic bishops was convened by Cardinal Cassidy and the Archbishop of Canterbury in Mississauga, Canada. Its purpose was to address the imperative for Christian reconciliation and healing in a broken and divided world at the beginning of a new millennium, to assess the progress made in Anglican – Roman Catholic relations and to chart a way forward for the future. The assembled bishops focused on the special relationship between the two Communions which was expressed in *Unitatis Redintegratio*, the decree on ecumenism of the Second Vatican Council: "Among those [communions separated at the time of the Reformation from the Roman See] in which Catholic traditions and institutions in part continue to exist, the Anglican Communion occupies a special place."[10]

9   The Common Declaration by Pope John Paul II and the Archbishop of Canterbury Dr George Carey, December 5, 1996, in *Information Service* 94 (1997/I), pp. 20–21.
10   *Unitatis Redintegratio*, n.13, in *Vatican Council II: The Conciliar and Post Conciliar Documents*, Austin Flannery ed. (Dublin: Dominican Publications, 1975): "*Inter eas, in quibus traditiones et structurae catholicae ex parte subsistere pergunt, locum specialem tenet Communio anglicana.*"

5.   As the bishops prayed together and meditated on Holy Scripture they realised afresh both the degree of spiritual communion they already shared in a common liturgical inheritance and also the pain of not receiving Holy Communion together at the Eucharist. As they reviewed the theological agreed statements of ARCIC and the official responses of the two Communions to that work, they noted "the very impressive degree of agreement in faith that already exists". The bishops were able to discern that, in spite of remaining differences, the faith shared by Anglicans and Roman Catholics "is not just formally established by our common baptism into Christ, but is even now a rich and life-giving, multifaceted communion".[11] As they reviewed together relations in the different regions of the world, they were encouraged by examples of collaboration, particularly in action for social justice and joint pastoral care. At the same time they noted that the degree of faith we currently share could allow us to join much more profoundly in common mission to our fragmented world, and that our disunity inevitably damages the mission of the Church. They called upon the churches to enter into a new stage in our relations, marked by "a communion of joint commitment to our common mission in the world (cf. John 17.23)".[12]

6.   In recognising this degree of communion, the bishops at Mississauga set out a vision of the way in which a new relationship might be marked:

> We believe that now is the appropriate time for the authorities of our two Communions to recognise and endorse this new stage through the signing of a Joint Declaration of Agreement. This Agreement would set out: our shared goal of visible unity; an acknowledgement of the consensus in faith that we have reached, and a fresh commitment to share together in common life and witness.[13]

---

11   *Communion in Mission* (*Information Service* 104 [2000/III], pp. 138–39), nn.4–5.
12   *Ibid.* n.8.
13   *Ibid.* n.10.

Since this meeting, however, the Churches of the Anglican Communion have entered into a period of dispute occasioned by the episcopal ordination of a person living in an openly acknowledged committed same-sex relationship and the authorisation of public Rites of Blessing for same-sex unions. These matters have intensified reflection on the nature of the relationship between the churches of the Communion. The Anglican Communion has acted to address these difficulties, notably through the *Windsor Report* of 2004. It is noteworthy that Anglicans have looked for the positive assistance of their ecumenical partners including the Catholic Church in this process.[14] In addition, ecumenical relationships have become more complicated as proposals within the Church of England have focused attention on the issue of the ordination of women to the episcopate which is an established part of ministry in some Anglican provinces.

7. This present context, which adds to existing differences between our two Communions, is not the appropriate time to enter the new formal stage of relationship envisaged by the bishops at Mississauga. Nevertheless it must be acknowledged that the progress towards agreement in faith achieved through the theological dialogue has been substantial, but that in the past four decades we have only just begun to give tangible expression to the incontrovertible elements of shared faith. Even in a time of uncertainty, the mission given us by Christ obliges and compels us to seek to engage more deeply and widely in a partnership in mission, coupled with common witness and joint prayer.

8. In developing the text of this statement, the International Anglican – Roman Catholic Commission for Unity and Mission (IARCCUM) is well aware that it has not answered the full

---

14   Cf. the report of an *ad hoc* sub-commission of IARCCUM, 'Ecclesiological Reflections on the Current Situation in the Anglican Communion in the Light of ARCIC', in *Information Service* 119 (2005/III), pp. 102–115; letter of Cardinal Kasper to the Archbishop of Canterbury, December 17, 2004, reprinted in *Information Service* 118 (2005/I-II), pp. 38–39.

challenge extended by the bishops at Mississauga; but ever mindful that Christ continues to urge us towards unity, the Commission has sought to undertake what is appropriate in the present context. In order to renew the enthusiasm which was shared at Mississauga, to transmit it to the future and to give common witness in our secularised societies, we must be honest in addressing and seeking to overcome recent problems. We believe that this is possible when we hold to our rich common heritage and the results already achieved through our dialogue. In addition to all we can and must do, we trust the Holy Spirit that the One who initiated our pilgrimage to unity and common mission will bring it to fulfilment.

9. The following text offers an honest appraisal of what has been achieved in the dialogue: discerning those doctrinal elements over which there is a readiness in both of our Communions to see in ARCIC's work a faithful expression of what the Church of Christ teaches; and candidly pointing to remaining difficulties, thus identifying where further theological work is necessary. In the text, these issues calling for further exploration have been placed in clearly identifiable boxes.

10. From the first beginnings of our theological dialogue, Anglican – Roman Catholic relations have consistently embraced the notion of unity by stages, acknowledging that our churches would need to grow gradually into the full communion which Christ desires for us, and trusting that the Holy Spirit would guide this process. While this may not be the moment to initiate a formal new stage in our relations, we believe that it is the time to bridge the gap between the elements of faith we hold in common and the tangible expression of that shared belief in our ecclesial lives. The final section of this document therefore proposes some specific steps to deepen our fellowship in life and mission which we believe are responsibly open for us and would be appropriate for us to take in the present context.

The faith we hold in common

1. Belief in God as Trinity

11. Together the Roman Catholic Church and the Churches of the Anglican Communion believe that Christian life is begun in the waters of Baptism. We agree that this sacrament involves a threefold profession of faith in God who is Father, Son and Holy Spirit, the Most Holy Trinity. The threefold profession, both at Baptism and also on those great occasions, above all at Easter, when baptismal promises are renewed, corresponds to the three clauses of the Apostles' Creed. Our full recognition of one another's Baptism is itself the basis of the growing communion between us.

12. Anglicans and Roman Catholics rejoice to be able to affirm as one:

I believe in God, the Father almighty,
creator of heaven and earth.
I believe in Jesus Christ, his only Son, our Lord.
He was conceived by the power of the Holy Spirit
and born of the Virgin Mary.
He suffered under Pontius Pilate, was crucified, died and was buried.
He descended to the dead.
On the third day he rose again.
He ascended into heaven, and is seated at the right hand of the Father.
He will come again to judge the living and the dead.
I believe in the Holy Spirit, the holy catholic Church,
the communion of saints, the forgiveness of sins,
the resurrection of the body, and the life everlasting. Amen.

13. We confess together that we are the graced recipients of the wholly unmerited gift of God's self-revelation in Christ. Our profession of faith springs from this gift, as also does our

solemn responsibility to go out and share what we have received (cf. Matthew 10.8; 28.18–20). We proclaim that Christ is the image of the invisible God (Colossians 1.15). He, the unique mediator between God and humanity, took flesh, suffered and died on the Cross for us, and was raised to life by the Father through the power of the Spirit, so that we in turn might have life through the same Spirit (cf. Romans 8.11), partake in the divine nature (cf. 2 Peter 1.4), and so reflect the glory of God (cf. 2 Corinthians 3.18).[15] By the will of the Father and the work of the Holy Spirit, Christ has redeemed the world once and for all (cf. Colossians 1.20–22). We are deeply united in joyful thanksgiving to the living God, Father, Son and Holy Spirit. In liturgical celebrations, we regularly make the same trinitarian profession of faith in the form of the Apostles' Creed or the Nicene–Constantinopolitan Creed.

14. We believe that the divine life is one of communion (in Greek, *koinonia*), and that the Church is a communion by participation in the eternal communion of the Son with the Father in the Holy Spirit.[16] The 'communion of saints' we profess in the Apostles' Creed translates the Latin, *communio sanctorum*, which is simultaneously the communion of God's holy people (*sancti*) and their communion in God's holy gifts (*sancta*) of word and sacrament.[17] The Roman Catholic Church and the Anglican Communion can already recognise many of God's gifts in one another. This sharing in God's gifts already constitutes a bond of communion between us. We are called to live out that real but imperfect communion visibly, while striving ultimately for full visible unity.

---

15 Cf. ARCIC, *Salvation and the Church* (1987), n.1; our humanity is transformed, recreated, restored and perfected in Christ (*ibid.* nn.12, 13, 17, 19), purely by God's grace (*ibid.* nn.1, 3, 9, 19, 23–25, 27, 30).
16 Cf. ARCIC, *Church as Communion* (1991), n.6 ff.
17 *Salvation and the Church*, nn.1, 9, 11.

2. Church as Communion in Mission

15. "The purpose of God according to Holy Scripture is to gather the whole of creation under the Lordship of Jesus Christ in whom, by the power of the Holy Spirit, all are brought into communion with God (Ephesians 1). The Church is the foretaste of this communion with God and with one another."[18] Anglicans and Catholics in dialogue have come to agree that communion or *koinonia* is the term that most aptly expresses the mystery underlying the various New Testament images of the Church.[19] Union with God in Christ Jesus through the Spirit is the heart of Christian *koinonia*. The Son of God has taken to himself our human nature, and he has sent upon us his Spirit, who makes us so truly members of the body of Christ that we too are able to call God "*Abba*, Father" (Romans 8.15; Galatians 4.6). *Koinonia* with one another is entailed by our *koinonia* with God in Christ (cf. 1 John 1.1–4). This is the mystery of the Church.[20]

16. Moreover, we agree that this mystery requires visible expression.[21] The Church is intended to be the 'sacrament' of God's saving work, i.e. 'both sign and instrument'[22] of God's purpose in Christ, "to unite all things in him, things in heaven and things on earth" (Ephesians 1.10).[23] As the body of Christ the incarnate Son, who was sent into the world because God loves the world (cf. John 3.16–17), the Church itself is essentially sent on mission into the world. Its mission is rooted in the saving mission of the Son and the Spirit and is, indeed, a sacramental form of that divine mission.

---

18 *The Unity of the Church as* Koinonia: *Gift and Calling* ('The Canberra Statement', 1991), in *Growth in Agreement II*, J. Gros, H. Meyer and W. Rusch, eds, (Geneva/Grand Rapids: WCC Publications/Eerdmans, 2000), p. 937.

19 ARCIC, *The Final Report* (London: CTS/SPCK, 1981), Introduction, n.4.

20 *Ibid.* n.5; cf. *Church as Communion*, nn.8, 13, 43.

21 *Ibid.* n.7; cf. *Church as Communion*, n.43.

22 *Ibid.* n.7; cf. *Salvation and the Church*, nn.26–29; *Church as Communion*, nn.17, 19.

23 *Church as Communion*, nn.15, 35, 38.

17. The Church is, therefore, a communion in mission. It is
     precisely as communion that the Church is "sacrament of the
     merciful grace of God for all humankind"[24] and sent into the
     world. The Church's own unity is at once an experience of the
     mystery of the Kingdom and a Gospel witness (cf. Jesus' prayer,
     "that they may all be one . . . so that the world may believe",
     John 17.21). The Church's living of communion is therefore a
     vital part of its mission, and mission is harmed when
     communion is lacking. The Church announces what it is called
     to become,[25] and is already the community where salvation is
     offered and received. It is therefore an effective sign, given by
     God in the face of human sinfulness, division and alienation.[26]
     "Confessing that their communion signifies God's purpose for
     the whole human race, the members of the Church are called to
     give themselves in loving witness and service to their fellow
     human beings."[27]

18. As a foretaste of the Kingdom, the Church exists to announce
     the fullness of the Kingdom. The Holy Spirit who anoints and
     empowers the Church reveals to it the things to come (cf. John
     16.13). While also acting outside the community of Christians,
     the Spirit nurtures the new life of the Kingdom within the
     Church, where Christ is confessed explicitly,[28] and the Gospel
     becomes "a manifest reality".[29] The Church is called to be "a
     living expression of the Gospel, evangelised and evangelising,
     reconciled and reconciling, gathered together and gathering

---

24 *Ibid.* n.5. The Catholic Church made the same point in the 'Final Relatio' of
the Extraordinary Synod held in Rome in 1985 to celebrate the twentieth
anniversary of the ending of Vatican II: "The Church as communion is a
sacrament for the salvation of the world" (II, D, 1 in *L'Osservatore Romano*,
10 December 1985).

25 *The Final Report,* Introduction, n.7.

26 *Church as Communion,* n.19.

27 *Ibid.* n.22.

28 *Ibid.* n.22.

29 *Salvation and the Church,* n.28. Likewise, at Vatican II, the Catholic Church
stated: "The Church believes that it is led by the Spirit of the Lord who fills the
whole world" (*Gaudium et Spes* [Pastoral Constitution on the Church in the
Modern World], n.11). "Every benefit the people of God can confer on mankind
during its earthly pilgrimage is rooted in the Church's being the 'universal
sacrament of salvation', at once manifesting and actualising the mystery of God's
love for men" (*Gaudium et Spes,* n.45).

others".[30] "Christ's will and prayer are that his disciples should be one. Those who have received the same word of God and have been baptised in the same Spirit cannot, without disobedience, indefinitely acquiesce in a state of separation. Unity is of the essence of the Church, and since the Church is visible its unity also must be visible."[31] We are therefore irrevocably committed to the re-establishment of full visible unity.

19. Roman Catholics and Anglicans agree that the Eucharist is the effectual sign of *koinonia*, that the ministry of oversight (*episcope*) serves the *koinonia*, and that a ministry of primacy is a visible link and focus of *koinonia*.[32] We understand the Church to be a communion of local churches (dioceses).[33] A local church is "a gathering of the baptised brought together by the apostolic preaching, confessing the one faith, celebrating the one eucharist, and led by an apostolic ministry".[34] Amongst the diversity of local churches, unity and coherence are maintained by the common confession of the one apostolic faith, by a shared sacramental life, by a common ministry of oversight, with both collegial and primatial dimensions, and by joint ways of reaching decisions and giving authoritative teaching.[35] We agree that the one celebration of the Eucharist is the "pre-eminent expression and focus" of ecclesial communion.[36]

20. Within the context of our agreement on the nature of the Church and its mission, the question must be addressed: where is the Church actually to be found? Anglicans and Roman Catholics agree that there are essential elements, constitutive of ecclesial life, which must be "present and mutually recognised" in each local church, in order for there to be that "one visible

---

30   *Salvation and the Church*, n.28.
31   *The Final Report*, Introduction, n.9.
32   Cf. *ibid.* n.6.
33   Cf. also the expression, 'a body of churches' (*corpus Ecclesiarum*), used by Vatican II, *Lumen Gentium* (Dogmatic Constitution on the Church), n.23.
34   *Church as Communion*, n.43; cf. Acts 2.42.
35   *Ibid.* nn.39, 45.
36   *Ibid.* n.45, cf. n.24.

communion which God wills".[37] The degree of visible communion depends on the extent of our mutual recognition of the holy gifts and the essential constitutive elements of the Church in one another.

21. For Anglicans, the 1998 Lambeth Conference reaffirmed the 1888 Chicago–Lambeth Quadrilateral "as a basis on which Anglicans seek the full, visible unity of the Church" and also recognised it "as a statement of Anglican unity and identity".[38] This 'brief, shorthand expression of the features necessary for visible unity', which has also "served Anglicans well as the basis for ecumenical conversations", consists of the Holy Scriptures of the Old and New Testaments, the Apostles' and Nicene Creeds, the sacraments of Baptism and Eucharist, and the historic episcopate, these four being understood as "gifts for sustaining and nurturing a life of unity".[39] There is also general agreement that the maintenance of unity requires structures of communion. Meetings of bishops with a presiding bishop and councils or synods which bring together bishops, clergy and laity serve unity at the diocesan and provincial levels. The Archbishop of Canterbury, the Lambeth Conference of bishops, the Anglican Consultative Council, and the Primates' Meeting are called to serve the unity of the Communion at the world level. However, recognising that communion suffers when these instruments are neglected, Anglicans are giving renewed attention to the nature and role of their international structures.

22. For Catholics, the Second Vatican Council adopted an approach to the Church in terms of "the elements and endowments which together go to build up and give life to the Church itself".[40] The Council taught that fully incorporated into the Church are

---

37 Cf. *ibid.* nn.14, 43, 48.
38 Lambeth Conference, 1998, Resolution IV.2 (a).
39 'Called to be One': Section IV Report, in *The Official Report of the Lambeth Conference 1998* (Harrisburg: Morehouse Publishing, 1999), p. 233; cf. also Lambeth Conference, 1998, Resolution III.8.
40 Vatican II, *Unitatis Redintegratio*, n.3; cf. *Lumen Gentium*, n.8.

"those who, possessing the Spirit of Christ, accept all the means of salvation given to the Church together with her entire organisation, and who – by the bonds constituted by the profession of faith, the sacraments, ecclesiastical government, and communion – are joined in the visible structure of the Church of Christ, who rules her through the Supreme Pontiff and the bishops".[41] Because of the presence of all these elements, it taught that the Church of Christ that we profess in the Creed, to be one, holy, catholic and apostolic, "subsists in the Catholic Church, which is governed by the successor of Peter and by the bishops in communion with him".[42] The "fullness of grace and truth" and the "fullness of the means of salvation" have been entrusted to the Catholic Church,[43] a trust that can be obscured by "the weaknesses, mediocrity, sins and at times the betrayals of some of her children".[44] At the same time, the Council recognised that "some, even very many, of the most significant elements and endowments . . . can exist outside the visible boundaries of the Catholic Church";[45] "many elements of sanctification and truth are found outside its visible confines".[46] Among other elements, these include honour for sacred scripture, sincere religious zeal, baptism and other sacraments.[47] "To the extent that these elements are found in other Christian Communities, the one Church of Christ is effectively present in them."[48] Indeed, such elements constitute "the objective basis of the communion, albeit imperfect" which exists between the Catholic Church and other Christian communities.[49] There is prominent mention of the Petrine ministry in the teaching of Vatican II. Significantly, as in quotations above, it is associated

41 *Lumen Gentium*, n.14; cf. also n.15.
42 *Ibid.* n.8.
43 *Unitatis Redintegratio*, n.3.
44 Cf. Pope John Paul II's Encyclical Letter on ecumenism, *Ut Unum Sint* (1995), n.11.
45 *Unitatis Redintegratio*, n.3.
46 *Lumen Gentium*, n.8.
47 Cf. *Lumen Gentium*, n.15.
48 *Ut Unum Sint*, n.11.
49 *Ibid.*

with the ministry of the bishops. One of the landmark teachings of Vatican II was that bishops form a college in succession to the college of the apostles and that, "together with their head, the Supreme Pontiff, and never apart from him, they have supreme and full authority over the universal Church".[50]

23. While already we can affirm together that universal primacy, as a visible focus of unity, is "a gift to be shared", able to be "offered and received even before our Churches are in full communion",[51] nevertheless serious questions remain for Anglicans regarding the nature and jurisdictional consequences of universal primacy.[52]

24. Anglicans and Catholics share a considerable degree of agreement on the constitutive elements of visible communion. We agree that the ministry of oversight has "both collegial and primatial dimensions", and furthermore, that in the context of the communion of all the churches, the episcopal ministry of a universal primate finds its role as "the visible focus of unity".[53]

25. Our ecumenical effort is founded on the conviction that all of these gifts, "which come from Christ and lead back to him, belong by right to the one Church of Christ".[54] "Full unity will come about when we all share in the fullness of the means of salvation entrusted by Christ to his Church."[55] In our search for unity, the goal of the Roman Catholic Church and the Anglican Communion is to come together in a common confession of the apostolic faith and a shared sacramental life with a common ministry of oversight. The sharing of these inter-related elements will serve and strengthen the Church's witness in mission.

---

50 *Lumen Gentium*, n.22.
51 ARCIC, *The Gift of Authority* (1999), n.60.
52 Cf. ARCIC, *Authority in the Church II* (1981), nn.17–22.
53 *Church as Communion*, n.45.
54 *Unitatis Redintegratio*, n.3; cf. *Lumen Gentium*, n.8.
55 *Ut Unum Sint*, n.86.

3. The Living Word of God

26. Anglicans and Roman Catholics embrace a common Christian inheritance, shared for many centuries, "with its living traditions of liturgy, theology, spirituality, Church order, and mission".[56] We agree that the Church lives in a dynamic process of tradition, "communicating to each generation what was delivered once and for all to the apostolic community",[57] and that the Church is "servant and not master of what it has received".[58] Through many centuries beforehand, God prepared his people for the coming of Christ. The patriarchs and the prophets received and spoke the word of God in the Spirit, and then, in the fullness of time (Galatians 4.4), by the power of the same Spirit, the Word of God took flesh, was born of a woman, and accomplished his ministry.[59]

27. The Word who became flesh and dwelt among us is at the centre of what was transmitted from the beginning and what will be transmitted until the end,[60] and the Holy Spirit quickens the memory of the teaching and work of Christ and of his exaltation, of which the apostolic community was the first witness.[61] It is the living Word of God, together with the Spirit, who communicates God's invitation to communion to the whole world in every age.[62] Therefore, we rejoice to reaffirm that the Church's mission is most truly that of the Son and the Spirit.

---

56   *The Malta Report* (Report of the Anglican – Roman Catholic Joint Preparatory Commission, 1968; published in *The Final Report*, pp. 108–116), n.3.
57   *Ibid.* n.14. By convention, the capitalised word 'Tradition' refers to 'the Gospel itself, transmitted from generation to generation in and by the Church', indeed to 'Christ himself'; the uncapitalised word 'tradition' refers to 'the traditionary process', the handing on of the revealed truth; and the plural 'traditions' refers to the diversity of forms of expression and of confessional traditions; cf. Fourth World Conference on Faith and Order, *Montreal Report*, 1963, section II, n.39. By their very nature, traditions stand in need of regular scrutiny.
58   *Salvation and the Church*, n.27.
59   ARCIC, *Authority in the Church I: Elucidation* (1981), n.2.
60   *The Gift of Authority*, n.14.
61   *Church as Communion*, n.26.
62   *Ibid.* n.27.

Properly understood, tradition is itself an act of communion whereby the Spirit unites the local churches of our day with those that preceded them in the one apostolic faith.[63] The communion of the Church spans time and space.[64]

28. We agree that the revealed Word is "received and communicated through the life of the whole Christian community";[65] since the Holy Spirit is given to all the people of God, it is within the Church as a whole that the living memory of the faith is active.[66] Christians are together formed into the body of Christ by the Spirit for the praise and glory of God and to minister grace and communion to the world.

29. We exist as Christians by the Tradition of the Gospel, testified in Scripture, transmitted in and by the Church through the power of the Holy Spirit.[67] "Within Tradition the Scriptures occupy a unique and normative place and belong to what has been given once for all."[68] At a very early stage, by the guidance of the Holy Spirit, "the Church was led to acknowledge the canon of Scripture as both test and norm" in order to safeguard the authenticity of its memory.[69] Therefore the Scriptures as the uniquely inspired witness to divine revelation have a unique role in keeping alive the Church's memory of the teaching and work of Christ. We agree that the Church's teaching, preaching and action must constantly be measured against the Scriptures; however the manner in which we each understand the Scriptures as "test and norm" needs still more clarification.

30. In approaching Scripture, the Christian faithful draw upon the rich diversity of methods of reading and interpretation used

63   *The Gift of Authority*, n.16.
64   *Church as Communion*, n.31.
65   *The Gift of Authority*, n.14.
66   *Church as Communion*, n.29.
67   *Montreal Report* 1963 (*op. cit.*), Section II, n.45.
68   *The Gift of Authority*, n.19.
69   *Church as Communion*, n.26.

throughout the Church's history (e.g. historical–critical, exegetical, typological, spiritual, sociological, canonical). These methods, which all have value, have been developed in many different contexts of the Church's life, which need to be recalled and respected. Anglican – Roman Catholic dialogue in recent decades has itself been a context for the development of an ecumenical reading of Scripture that has consciously tried to get behind well-known controversies and to seek new shared insights concerning those things which have divided us.[70]

31. Effective preaching is indispensable in enabling the Scriptures to nourish the faithful and in communicating the living Word of God (cf. Romans 10.14–17). The responsibility to keep the community true to the apostolic faith, and transmit that faith to the Church of every age, is an essential element in the ministry of those who have oversight in the Church.[71] In order to sustain and promote the Church's mission[72] they exercise a ministry of memory, preaching, explaining and applying the truth of the Gospel.

32. Both Communions agree that, under the guidance of the Holy Spirit, the Tradition of the Gospel is alive in the Church, in continuity with the earliest Christian centuries when the apostolic witness, memory and interpretation took normative form in the canon of Scripture, and the first four councils formulated fundamental and binding doctrines of Christian faith. However, Anglicans and Roman Catholics diverge with regard to the status both of the councils held, and of the doctrines formulated, in the intervening centuries up to today. There are further divergences in the way in which teaching authority in the life of the Church is exercised and the authentic tradition is discerned (cf. paragraphs 69, 71 and 73–76 below).

---

70 Cf. ARCIC, *Mary: Grace and Hope in Christ* (2005), n.7, which explicitly states the Commission's intent to offer an 'ecclesial and ecumenical' reading of Scripture.
71 Cf. ARCIC, *Ministry and Ordination* (1973), n.10.
72 Cf. *Church as Communion*, n.32.

4. Baptism

33. Anglicans and Roman Catholics agree that they receive one
baptism, administered with water in the name of the Father, the
Son, and the Holy Spirit. We do this in obedience to the
command of the risen Lord (cf. Matthew 28.18–20). We
consider baptism a sacrament of initiation instituted by Jesus
Christ, by which we are incorporated into the life of his body,
the Church. Baptism is the sacrament of faith, through which a
person embraces the faith of the Church and is embraced by it.

34. Together with other Christians, we accept the meanings baptism
has in the Scriptures, and the tradition and practice of the early
Church.[73] By baptism, through faith, Christians are united with
Christ in his life, death and resurrection. Along with all our
human sinfulness, we are buried with Christ (cf. Romans
6.3–11) and raised to a new life, which begins here and now, in
the power of his resurrection.[74] Thus we believe this one
baptism is for the forgiveness of sins, including original sin, and
that we are pardoned, washed and cleansed by Christ, who
came into the world to save sinners. "Baptism is the
unrepeatable sacrament of justification and incorporation into
Christ (1 Corinthians 6.11, 12.12–13; Galatians 3.27)."[75]
Through baptism, by grace alone and not because of any merit
on our part, we put on Christ, and receiving his Spirit, we are
enabled to live a new life.

35. By the power of the indwelling Spirit, baptism initiates a
renewal of life and growth in holiness which God will bring to
completion in eternal life. What is given in baptism is the "first
instalment of the final consummation and the ground of the
believer's hope".[76] By this lifelong process of sanctification,

---

73 Cf. World Council of Churches, *Baptism, Eucharist and Ministry* [*BEM*],
Faith and Order Paper no.111 (Geneva: WCC Publications 1982), Baptism,
nn.1–23.
74 Cf. *ibid.* n.3.
75 *Salvation and the Church*, n.16.
76 *Ibid.*

believers "grow into conformity with Christ, the perfect image of God, until he appears and we shall be like him".[77]

36. We believe that all who are baptised are incorporated into the body of Christ, the Church. "Through baptism, Christians are brought into union with Christ, with each other and with the Church of every time and place."[78] This spiritual communion of the baptised receives necessary expression in a visible community, in which the Word of God is proclaimed afresh, the sacraments are celebrated, and the people of God receive pastoral oversight, so that the life of the Gospel and the mission flowing from it are lived out by the baptised.[79] Baptism into the Christian community is directed to the full expression of the new life received in Christ, as sin is overcome and God is served and glorified in Christ-like lives.

37. In both the Anglican Communion and the Roman Catholic Church, the sacramental process of Christian initiation also includes confirmation. Common to our understanding is that confirmation is an empowerment by the Holy Spirit for witness and mission, and a public manifestation of membership in the Body of Christ. The twentieth century saw a reappraisal in both the Roman Catholic Church and the Anglican Communion of the relationship between Baptism, Confirmation and participation in Holy Communion. In both traditions, it is now widespread practice to admit children to Communion at the age of reason.

38. The Anglican Communion and the Catholic Church recognise the baptism each confers. Anglicans and Catholics therefore regard our common baptism as the basic bond of unity between us,[80] even as we recognise that the fullness of eucharistic communion to which baptism should lead is impeded by

---

77   *Ibid.* n.17.
78   *BEM*, Baptism, n.6.
79   Cf. *Church as Communion*, nn.15, 19.
80   Cf. *ibid.* n.50, quoting the Common Declaration of Pope John Paul II and Archbishop Robert Runcie, 2 October, 1989.

disagreement concerning some of the elements of faith and practice which we acknowledge are necessary for full, visible communion. Nevertheless, we recognise that this incompleteness constitutes an imperative: Anglicans and Catholics are committed to overcoming by God's grace all the divisions that still hinder the fullness of eucharistic and ecclesial communion. Our fundamental baptismal communion gives us the shared responsibility to witness as fully as possible to the Gospel of Christ before the world and to show forth the new life lived by the body of Christ, with the liberation and renewal it brings.

5. Eucharist

39. Anglicans and Catholics agree that the full participation in the Eucharist, together with Baptism and Confirmation, completes the sacramental process of Christian initiation.[81] The Eucharist is a gift received from the Lord himself, and celebrated in obedience to his command until he comes again (cf. 1 Corinthians 11.23–25; Matthew 26.26–29; Mark 14.22–25; Luke 22.14–20; John 6.53–58). The visible communion of Christ's body, entered through baptism, is nourished, deepened, and expressed in the eucharistic communion when believers eat and drink and receive the body and blood of Christ. When his people are gathered at the Eucharist to commemorate Christ's saving acts for our redemption, he makes present and effective among us the eternal benefits of his victory and elicits and renews his people's response of faith, thanksgiving and self-surrender.[82] The identity of the Church as Christ's body is expressed and visibly proclaimed by its being centred in the partaking of Christ's body and blood in the Eucharist.[83]

40. We agree that the Eucharist is the memorial (*anamnesis*) of the crucified and risen Christ, of the entire work of reconciliation God has accomplished in him.[84] By memorial, Anglicans and

---

81 Cf. *BEM*, Baptism, n.20.
82 Cf. ARCIC, *Eucharistic Doctrine* (1971), n.3.
83 *Ibid.*
84 Cf. ARCIC, *Eucharistic Doctrine: Elucidation*, (1979), n.5; also 1 Corinthians 11.24–25; Luke 22.19.

Catholics both intend not merely a calling to mind of what God has done in the past but an effectual sacramental proclamation, which through the action of the Holy Spirit makes present what has been accomplished and promised once-and-for-all. In this sense, then, there is only one historical, unrepeatable sacrifice, offered once for all by Christ and accepted once for all by the Father, which cannot be repeated or added to.[85] The eucharistic memorial, however, makes present this once-and-for-all sacrifice of Christ. It is therefore possible to say that "the Eucharist is a sacrifice in the sacramental sense, provided that it is clear that this is not a repetition of the historical sacrifice."[86] "In the Eucharistic Prayer, the Church continues to make a perpetual memorial of Christ's death, and his members, united with God and one another, give thanks for all his mercies, entreat the benefits of his passion on behalf of the whole Church, participate in these benefits, and enter into the movement of his self-offering."[87] The action of the Church in the eucharistic celebration "adds nothing to the efficacy of Christ's sacrifice on the cross" but is rather a fruit of that sacrifice. In the eucharistic celebration Christ's one sacrifice is made present for us.[88]

41.   Anglicans and Catholics believe in the real presence of Christ in the Eucharist. The real communion with Christ crucified and risen presupposes his true presence, which is "effectually signified by the bread and wine which, in this mystery, become his body and blood."[89] "What is here affirmed is a sacramental presence in which God uses the realities of this world to convey the realities of the new creation: bread for this life becomes the bread of eternal life. Before the Eucharistic Prayer, to the question: 'What is that?', the believer answers: 'It is bread'. After the Eucharistic Prayer, to the same question he answers: 'It is truly the body of Christ, the Bread of Life.'"[90] While Christ is present and active in a variety of ways in the entire eucharistic

---

85 Cf. *Eucharistic Doctrine*, n.5.
86 *Eucharistic Doctrine: Elucidation*, n.5.
87 *Eucharistic Doctrine*, n.5.
88 Cf. *Eucharistic Doctrine: Elucidation*, n.5.
89 *Eucharistic Doctrine*, n.6.
90 *Eucharistic Doctrine: Elucidation*, n.6.

celebration, so that his presence is not limited to the consecrated elements,[91] the bread and wine are not empty signs: Christ's body and blood become really present and are really given in these elements.[92]

42. The real presence of Christ depends not on an individual believer's faith but on the power of the Holy Spirit, whom the Church invokes in the liturgy in order to receive the Lord's real gift of himself.[93] Nevertheless, Anglicans and Catholics agree that faith is required in order that, partaking of the sacrament of the Lord's real presence, a life-giving encounter may result.[94] "The bread and wine become the sacramental body and blood of Christ in order that the Christian community may become more truly what it already is, the body of Christ."[95]

43. We agree that the Eucharist is the "meal of the Kingdom",[96] in which the Church gives thanks for all the signs of the coming Kingdom. By the transforming action of the Spirit of God the elements of bread and wine, fruits of the first creation, become an anticipation of the joys of the age to come, "pledges and first-fruits of the new heaven and new earth",[97] and a foretaste of the Kingdom.[98] Reconciled in the Eucharist, the members of the body of Christ are called to be "servants of reconciliation among men and women and witnesses of the joy of the resurrection"[99] which breaks into our world.

44. Anglicans and Roman Catholics agree that every celebration of the Eucharist has to do with the whole Church, and that the whole Church is involved in each local celebration. The communion established in the body of Christ is a communion

---

91 Cf. *Eucharistic Doctrine*, n.7; *Eucharistic Doctrine: Elucidation*, n.6.
93 Cf. *Eucharistic Doctrine*, n.8.
94 *Ibid.*
95 Cf. *ibid.*; also *BEM*, Eucharist, n.13.
96 *Eucharistic Doctrine: Elucidation*, n.6.
96 Cf. *BEM*, Eucharist, nn.22–26.
97 *Eucharistic Doctrine*, n.11.
98 Cf. *BEM*, Eucharist, n.6.
99 *Ibid.* n.24.

with all Christians of all times and places.[100] They also agree that only bishops and episcopally ordained and authorised priests preside at the Eucharist.

45. Anglicans and Roman Catholics hold that there is an inextricable link between Eucharist and Ministry. Without recognition and reconciliation of ministries, therefore (cf. paragraphs 60 to 61 below), it is not possible to realise the full impact of our common understanding of the Eucharist.

46. Anglicans and Catholics acknowledge that there is an intrinsic relationship between sharing the Eucharist and full ecclesial communion, but diverge on the way in which that is expressed on the way to full communion. Churches of the Anglican Communion and Roman Catholic Church therefore have different disciplines for eucharistic sharing.

47. The Catholic Church regards eucharistic sharing by those not yet in full ecclesial communion as something exceptional, limited to particular cases of spiritual need.[101] Moreover, it does not permit the Catholic faithful to receive the Eucharist from, nor Catholic clergy to concelebrate with, those whose ministry has not been officially recognised by the Catholic Church.[102]

48. Anglican provinces regularly admit to communion baptised believers who are communicant members from other Christian communities. In certain circumstances, Anglicans permit eucharistic sharing with other churches where there is sufficient agreement in faith and commitment to shared life. Some Anglican Churches recognise that the sacramental ministry of women clergy is not accepted by some of their faithful, and make provision accordingly, although this results in the impairment of full eucharistic communion.

---

100   Cf. *ibid.* n.19.
101   Cf. Pontifical Council for Promoting Christian Unity, *Directory for the Application of Principles and Norms on Ecumenism*, Vatican City, 1993, nn.104, 122–123, 129–131.
102   Cf. *ibid.* n.132.

49. Anglicans and Roman Catholics reserve the sacrament for those unable to attend the eucharistic celebration. This is understood as an extension of the celebration. Adoration of Christ in the reserved sacrament is encouraged in the Roman Catholic Church. While it is also practised in some Anglican churches, there are some Anglicans who would find difficulty in these devotional practices because it is feared that they obscure the true goal of the sacrament.[103]

6. Ministry

50. Anglicans and Roman Catholics agree that Christ entrusts his own ministry to the whole Church as his Body; his ministry is the source and model from which all ministry flows and takes its shape.[104] The Holy Spirit gives to every baptised person gifts (charisms) to be used in the service of the Christian community and in the service of the world and its needs. All are called to offer their lives as a "living sacrifice" (Romans 12.1) and to pray for the Church and for the world.[105]

51. Within the community of the Church, the ordained ministry is part of God's design for his people. Ordained ministry relates both to the ministry of Christ and to the ministry of the whole people of God.[106] In the early Church, the Apostles exercised a ministry, unique and unrepeatable, which remains of fundamental significance for the Church of all ages.[107] Ordained ministers have special care and responsibility for continuing the teaching and mission of the Apostles and for symbolising and maintaining apostolicity, which is a mark of the whole Church.

---

103 Cf. *Clarifications; Eucharistic Doctrine: Elucidation*, n.9.
104 Cf. *Ministry and Ordination*, n.3.
105 Cf. *ibid.* n.17.
106 Cf. *ibid.* n.3.
107 Cf. *ibid.* n.4.

52. We agree that the providential threefold ordering of the ministry of bishop, presbyter (priest) and deacon emerged from the patterns of ministry in the New Testament, under the guidance of the Holy Spirit, very early in the history of the Church. Both of our Communions have retained the threefold ministry and intend to be faithful to that pattern.

53. Christ called the Apostles, and, in and through the Church, continues to call people to serve in the apostolic ministry. "Ordination denotes entry into this apostolic and God-given ministry."[108] The act of ordination is a sign of the apostolicity and continuity of the Church.[109] It is a sign of God's fidelity to the Church and of the Church's intention to be faithful to the Apostles' teaching and mission. In the sacramental act the bishop prays God to grant the gift of the Holy Spirit on those being ordained and lays hands on the candidates as the outward sign of the gift bestowed. Thus their vocation is from Christ and the qualification for the exercise of ministry is the gift of the Holy Spirit. Both Anglicans and Roman Catholics "affirm the pre-eminence of baptism and the eucharist as sacraments necessary to salvation. This does not diminish their understanding of the sacramental nature of ordination."[110] "Because ministry is in and for the community and because ordination is an act in which the whole Church of God is involved, the prayer and laying on of hands take place within the context of the eucharist."[111] Ordination is unrepeatable within both our Communions.

54. In both Communions presbyters and deacons are ordained by the bishop. In the ordination of a presbyter, the bishop is joined by presbyters in the laying on of hands, signifying the shared nature of the commission entrusted to the candidate. In the ordination of a new bishop, at least three bishops lay hands on the candidate, signifying that the new bishop and the local

---

108   *Ibid.* n.14.
109   Cf. *ibid.*
110   *Ministry and Ordination: Elucidation* (1979), n.3.
111   *Ministry and Ordination*, n.14.

church are within the communion of the churches. "Their participation also ensures the historical continuity of this church with the apostolic church and of its bishop with the original apostolic ministry."[112] The communion of the churches in mission, faith and holiness through time and space is thus symbolised and maintained in the bishop. Ordination is understood by both Communions as being in the succession of the Apostles, within the apostolicity of the whole Church.[113]

55. We agree that those who are ordained have responsibility for the ministry of Word and Sacrament. An essential element in the ordained ministry is the responsibility for oversight (*episcope*), to ensure that the Church lives in fidelity to the apostolic faith and to transmit it to the next generation.[114] The fullness of the ministry of oversight is entrusted to the episcopate, which has the responsibility of maintaining and expressing the unity of the Church and leading it in mission.[115] Consulting the faithful is an integral aspect of episcopal oversight.[116] Within a diocese the ministry of oversight is exercised by the bishop, and in the service of the communion of all the local churches, by bishops collegially. In their dioceses, when they come together regionally, and at a world-level, bishops have a special role in keeping the Church true to apostolic teaching and mission in conformity to the mind of Christ. Priests are associated with the bishop in the exercise of oversight and in the ministry of the Word and Sacraments, presiding at the Eucharist and pronouncing absolution.[117] Deacons are associated with bishops and presbyters in the ministry of Word and Sacrament. They have a special responsibility in collaboration with the bishops in the Church's ministry of outreach.

---

112   *Ibid.* n.16.
113   Cf. *Ibid.* n.15.
114   Cf. *Ibid.* n.9.
115   Cf. *Church as Communion,* n.45.
116   Cf. *The Gift of Authority,* n.38.
117   Cf. *Ministry and Ordination,* n.9.

56. The Anglican Communion and the Roman Catholic Church affirm the priesthood of bishops and presbyters, believing it to be related to the priesthood of Christ and the priesthood of the whole people of God.[118] The priesthood of Christ is unique. He is our High Priest who has reconciled humanity with the Father. All priesthood derives from his and is wholly dependent upon it. The priesthood of the whole people of God (cf. 1 Peter 2.5) is the consequence of incorporation by baptism into Christ and looks forward to their reign with Christ (cf. Revelation 5.10, 20.6).[119]

57. The ordained ministry is called priestly because it brings the whole of the Gospel to all the people for their salvation, so that they may be able to worship the true God (Romans 15.16). The ordained ministry is called priestly also because, in the celebration of the Eucharist as the memorial of Christ's sacrifice, the ordained ministry has a particular sacramental configuration with Christ as High Priest who continues to make intercession for us (Hebrews 7.25).[120] "At the eucharist Christ's people do what he commanded in memory of himself and Christ unites them sacramentally with himself in his self-offering. But in this action it is only the ordained minister who presides at the eucharist, in which, in the name of Christ and on behalf of his Church, the president recites the narrative of the institution of the Last Supper, and invokes the Holy Spirit upon the gifts. The word priesthood is used by way of analogy when it is applied to the people of God [the common priesthood] and to the ordained ministry. These are two distinct realities which relate, each in its own way, to the high priesthood of Christ, the unique priesthood of the new covenant . . ."[121]

58. The priesthood of the ordained ministry cannot be derived from the congregation. It is a distinct vocation, and not an enhancement of the common priesthood. But the common priesthood and the ministerial priesthood are nevertheless

---

118 Cf. *Ministry and Ordination*, n.13 and *BEM*, Ministry, n.17.
119 *Ministry and Ordination: Elucidation*, n.2.
120 Cf. *ibid.*
121 *Ibid.*

interrelated. The minister, though not the delegate of the congregation, does act in its name and focuses thereby its offering of worship. Only bishops and episcopally ordained and authorised priests preside at the Eucharist.

59. Roman Catholics and Anglicans share this agreement concerning the ministry of the whole people of God, the distinctive ministry of the ordained, the threefold ordering of the ministry, its apostolic origins, character and succession, and the ministry of oversight.

60. In his Apostolic Letter on Anglican Orders, *Apostolicae Curae* (1896), Pope Leo XIII ruled against the validity of Anglican Orders.[122] The question of validity remains a fundamental obstacle to the recognition of Anglican ministries by the Catholic Church. In the light of the agreements on the Eucharist and ministry set out both in the ARCIC statements and in the official responses of both Communions, there is evidence that we have a common intention in ordination and in the celebration of the Eucharist. This awareness would have to be part of any fresh evaluation of Anglican Orders.

61. The twentieth century saw much discussion across the whole Christian family on the question of the ordination of women. The Roman Catholic Church points to the unbroken tradition of the Church in not ordaining women. Indeed, Pope John Paul II expressed the conviction that "the Church has no authority whatsoever to confer priestly ordination on women".[123] After careful reflection and debate, a growing number of Anglican Churches have proceeded to ordain women to the presbyterate and some also to the episcopate.[124] They have done so, despite

---

122   The Archbishops of Canterbury and York addressed and rejected these arguments in their response *Saepius Officio* (1897).

123   Apostolic Letter of Pope John Paul II, *Ordinatio Sacerdotalis*, 1994, n.4.

124   At present 14 of the 38 provinces of the Anglican Communion have legislation in place to enable the ordination of women to the diaconate, the presbyterate and the episcopate. A further 12 provinces ordain women to the diaconate and presbyterate, and three provinces ordain women to the diaconate only.

sometimes strong differences of belief within those provinces, in the conviction that there are no theological objections to such a development, and that they are not departing from the traditional understanding of apostolic ministry nor the nature of ministry as set forth in the ARCIC statements.[125]

7. Authority in the Church

62. Anglicans and Roman Catholics agree that the primary authority for all Christians is Jesus Christ himself. "To him God has given all authority in heaven and on earth."[126] To follow Christ is to be set under the authority of Christ. The authority of the Church is derived from and wholly dependent upon the authority of Christ (cf. Matthew 11.27, 28.18ff.). "This is Christian authority: when Christians so act and speak, men perceive the authoritative word of Christ."[127] "It is in conformity with the mind and example of Christ that the Church is called to exercise authority (cf. Luke 22.24–27; John 13.14–15; Philippians 2.1–11)."[128] His authority "was demonstrated by his self-giving service in sacrificial love (cf. Mark 10.45)."[129]

63. Christ entrusts his authority to the Church, both to keep the Church mindful of God's purpose in creation and redemption, and also to help the Church respond faithfully to that purpose.[130] Moreover, authority has "a radically missionary

---

125 *Ministry Elucidation* n.5 reads: "While the Commission realizes that the ordination of women has created for the Roman Catholic Church a new and grave obstacle to the reconciliation of our communions (cf. Letter of Pope Paul VI to Archbishop Donald Coggan, 23 March 1976, AAS 68), it believes that the principles upon which its doctrinal agreement rests are not affected by such ordinations; for it was concerned with the origin and nature of the ordained ministry and not with the question who can or cannot be ordained. Objections, however substantial, to the ordination of women are of a different kind from objections raised in the past against the validity of Anglican Orders in general."
126 ARCIC, *Authority in the Church I* (1976), n.1; cf. Matthew 28.18.
127 *Ibid.* n.3.
128 *The Gift of Authority,* n.5.
129 *Ibid.* n.9.
130 Cf. *ibid.* nn.7–13.

dimension". "Authority is exercised within the Church for the sake of those outside it, that the Gospel may be proclaimed 'in power and in the Holy Spirit and with full conviction' (1Thessalonians 1.5)."[131]

64. Changing situations provide fresh challenges to the Gospel. Every generation is called to translate the Gospel prophetically. This dynamic process of communicating to each generation what was delivered once for all to the apostolic community is what is known as tradition, which is far more than the transmission of true propositions concerning salvation. This handing on (*traditio*) involves stating the Gospel in new ways. Yet such restatement must be consonant with the apostolic witness recorded in the Scriptures: within Tradition the Scriptures are uniquely authoritative.[132]

65. The Gospel is only fully understood in the Church. God's revelation has been entrusted to a community, which means that the whole people of God has the responsibility for discerning and communicating God's Word.[133] Within the 'symphony' of the whole people of God, everyone has a part to play – those with the ministry of oversight, the theologians and all the people of God.[134]

66. Bishops have a vital role in the process of discernment, bearing a special responsibility for promoting truth and discerning error and for preserving and promoting communion; but this is never exercised apart from the whole body of the faithful.[135] The interaction of bishop and people in this exercise of discernment and teaching is a safeguard of Christian life and fidelity. Discernment involves both heeding and sifting in order to assist the people of God in understanding, articulating and applying their faith.[136] The bishop's authority necessarily includes

---

131   *Ibid.* n.32.
132   Cf. *Authority in the Church I*, n.15 and *The Gift of Authority*, n.19.
133   *The Gift of Authority*, n.28.
134   Cf. *Ibid.* nn.28, 30.
135   Cf. *Authority in the Church I*, n.18.
136   Cf. *ibid.* and *Church as Communion*, n.32.

responsibility for making and implementing the decisions that are required for the sake of *koinonia*.[137]

67. At ordination, bishops receive not only responsibility for their local church but also a share in collegial responsibility for the wider community. "Bishops meet together collegially, not as individuals but as those who have authority within and for the synodal life of the local churches . . . When bishops take counsel together they seek both to discern and to articulate the *sensus fidelium* as it is present in the local church and in the wider communion of churches."[138] "The duty of maintaining the Church in truth is one of the essential functions of the episcopal college . . . The exercise of this teaching authority requires that what it teaches be faithful to Holy Scripture and consistent with apostolic Tradition."[139] "The challenge and responsibility for those with authority within the Church is so to exercise their ministry that they promote the unity of the whole Church in faith and life in a way that enriches rather than diminishes the legitimate diversity of local churches."[140]

68. We are agreed that no local church is self-sufficient. Various structures and practices are needed to maintain and manifest the communion of the local churches and sustain them in fidelity to the Gospel. These include local, provincial, world-wide and ecumenical synods and councils.[141] Anglicans and Roman Catholics agree that from New Testament times (cf. Acts 15.6–29), the Church has sought through collegial and conciliar gatherings to be obedient to Christ in fidelity to its vocation.

69. Anglicans and Roman Catholics agree that councils can be recognised as authoritative when they express the common faith and mind of the Church, consonant with Scripture and the apostolic Tradition.[142] Those councils up to modern times which

---

137 *The Gift of Authority*, n.36.
138 *Ibid.* n.38.
139 *Ibid.* n.44.
140 *Ibid.* n.33.
141 Cf. *ibid.* n.37.
142 Cf. *Authority in the Church I*, n.9.

the Catholic Church describes as 'ecumenical' are understood as having a binding character, and are for Roman Catholics an authoritative expression of the living tradition.[143] Anglicans historically have only recognised the binding authority of the first four ecumenical councils. While they affirm some of the content of successive councils, they believe that only those decisions which can be demonstrated from Scripture are binding on the faithful.

70. The communion of the Church requires a ministry of primacy at every level of the Church's life as a visible link and focus of its communion.[144] From early times an ordering developed among the bishops, whereby the bishops of prominent sees exercised a distinctive ministry of unity, as the first among the bishops of their regions. They acted not in isolation from but in collegial association with other bishops. Primacy and collegiality are complementary dimensions of *episcope*, exercised within the life of the whole Church. (Anglicans recognise the ministry of the Archbishop of Canterbury in precisely this way.)

71. The office of a universal primate is a special and particular case of that care for universal communion proper to the episcopal office itself. "The only see which makes any claim to universal primacy and which has exercised and still exercises such *episcope* is the see of Rome, the city where Peter and Paul died."[145] The Roman Catholic Church teaches that the ministry of the Bishop of Rome as universal primate is in accordance with Christ's will for the Church and an essential element for maintaining it in unity and truth. Anglicans rejected the jurisdiction of the Bishop of Rome as universal primate in the sixteenth century. Today, however, some Anglicans are beginning to see the potential value of a ministry of universal primacy, which would be exercised by the Bishop of Rome, as a sign and focus of unity within a re-united Church.[146]

---

143   Cf. *Authority in the Church I*, n.19, fn.2.
144   Cf. *Final Report*, Introduction, n.6.
145   *Authority in the Church I*, n.23.
146   Cf. *Authority in the Church II*, n.9.

72. We agree that the Church, "pillar and bulwark of the truth" (1 Timothy 3.15), is indefectible. The Church is confident that the Holy Spirit will effectually enable it to fulfil its mission so that it will neither lose its essential character nor fail to reach its goal.[147]

73. Anglicans and Roman Catholics share a considerable agreement on authority in the Church, although there are a number of remaining issues, including the binding authority of ecumenical councils, and the infallibility of the teaching office of the Church. Anglicans and Catholics continue to reflect upon the relationship between local and universal in the life of the Church, and in particular: on the place and authority of regional and national structures; on the place and role of the laity at every level of the Church's life, particularly in relation to the councils and synods of the Church; on the relationship between collegial and synodical gatherings; and on the place of reception in discerning the mind of Christ for the Church.

74. The question of whether the Anglican Communion is open to instruments of oversight which would allow decisions to be reached which in certain circumstances would bind the members of every province is an important and topical one. In turn, it has been asked whether in the Catholic Church enough provision has been made to ensure consultation between the Bishop of Rome and the local churches prior to the making of important decisions affecting either a local church or the whole Church.

75. While some Anglicans are coming to value the ministry of the Bishop of Rome as a sign and focus of unity, there continue to be questions about whether the Petrine ministry as exercised by the Bishop of Rome exists within the Church by divine right; about the nature of papal infallibility; and about the jurisdiction ascribed to the Bishop of Rome as universal primate.[148]

---

147 *Authority in the Church II*, n.23.
148 Cf. *The Gift of Authority*, nn.56, 57.

76. Anglicans and Roman Catholics both believe in the indefectibility of the Church, that the Holy Spirit leads the Church into all truth. For Catholics, it is secured by the faith that in specific circumstances and under certain precise conditions, those with a ministry of oversight, assisted by the Holy Spirit, can come to a judgement regarding matters of faith or morals which is preserved from error. This is what is meant by the Church teaching infallibly. Anglicans, believing that the indefectibility of the Church is preserved by fidelity to the Scriptures, the catholic creeds, the sacraments and the ministry of bishops, do not assign an infallible ministry to any group or individual within its life. They hold that doctrine, however proposed or defined, must be received by the body of believers to whom it is addressed as consonant with Scripture and Tradition.[149]

8. Discipleship and Holiness

77. Anglicans and Roman Catholics teach that the Christian vocation is to holiness of life (cf. Exodus 9.6; Matthew 5.48), and that moral behaviour is integral to the maintenance of communion with the Holy Trinity, as well as to communion with the community of believers in the Church. We have received the same Gospel and are agreed that the Gospel we proclaim cannot be divorced from the life we live (cf. 1 John 3.18; James 2.20).[150] Our common acceptance of the same fundamental moral values, and the sharing of the same vision of humanity, created in the image of God and recreated in Christ, are constitutive elements of ecclesial communion and are essential for the visible communion of the Church.[151]

---

149   Cf. Section Report on 'Dogmatic and Pastoral Concerns', in *The Truth Shall Make You Free: The Lambeth Conference 1988* (London: Church House, 1988), p. 104.
150   Cf. ARCIC, *Life in Christ: Morals, Communion and the Church* (1994), n.2.
151   Cf. *Church as Communion*, nn.44, 45.

78. We hold that the reality of createdness sets humanity in a relationship of interdependence with all creation and we affirm that the material order of creation may be caught up into and transfigured by the work of the Holy Spirit as an effective channel of his grace and love.

79. We affirm the dignity of the human person, male and female, created by God for communion with God. No matter what differences exist between people, we agree that all persons share equal dignity as creatures of God. From this flow the basic human rights to such necessities of life as food, clothing, shelter, education, work, freedom of religious expression and freedom to participate in the shaping of society. Our common tradition balances the dignity and rights of the individual with the good of the whole community. We agree that human freedom is a freedom of responsiveness and interdependence. Human persons are created for communion, and communion involves responsibility, in relation to society and creation as well as to God.[152] Living out the Gospel includes living in a relationship of justice and love with our neighbours, and requires us to contribute to the common good as well as to benefit from it. The call to follow Christ's example of self-giving love is sometimes a call to renounce what is rightfully ours in order to respond to a greater need of others in the human community.[153]

80. We agree that growth in Christ, for believers and for the believing community, arises from a response to the grace of God and is to be shaped according to the mind of Christ. The fidelity of the Church to the mind of Christ involves a continuous process of listening, learning, reflecting and teaching. In this process each member of the community has a part to play. Each person has to learn to reflect and act according to an informed conscience. Learning and teaching are a shared discipline, in which the faithful seek to discover together what obedience to the gospel of grace and the law of love entails amidst the moral perplexities of the world.[154]

---

152 Cf. *Life in Christ*, n.7.
153 *Church as Communion*, n.15.
154 Cf. *ibid.* n.29.

81. We agree that the context in which the Church is called to witness and exercise its ministry of healing, forgiveness and reconciliation, is marked by fragility and sin. Where there is moral failure, the Church strives to call forth repentance and makes every effort to restore sinners to the life of grace in the community and to proclaim forgiveness. We agree that the Church is a community with a vital two-fold ministry of reconciliation: it is a community in which the reconciliation that comes from God in Christ can be experienced by its members, and also a community that should promote reconciliation in every possible way in the world (cf. 2 Corinthians 18–21). Both Anglicans and Catholics acknowledge that private confession before a priest is a means of grace and an effective declaration of the forgiveness of Christ in response to repentance.

82. Throughout its history the Church has sought to be faithful in following Christ's command to heal, and this has inspired countless acts of ministry in medical and hospital care. Alongside this physical ministry, both traditions have continued to exercise the sacramental ministry of anointing. Within the Roman Catholic tradition, the act of anointing became especially associated with the rites administered to the Christian departing this life. But in recent years, there has been an increasing practice of anointing of the sick. Anglicans also have rediscovered the value of this sacramental action as an effective means of proclaiming the wider healing ministry of the Church.

83. Anglicans and Roman Catholics share similar ways of moral reasoning. We recognise the normative authority of Scripture and rely on a shared tradition which appeals to natural law and pays attention to the wisdom in the order of creation.[155]

84. The teaching of Anglicans and Roman Catholics is united or compatible on many matters of social ethics, for example, on war and peace. We agree that war as a method of settling international disputes is incompatible with the teaching and

---

155   Cf. *Life in Christ*, n.9.

example of our Lord Jesus Christ.[156] There has also been consistency in the application of this teaching to specific conflicts and a common use of insights drawn from theories of 'just war'. There is also consistency in our respective teaching regarding freedom and justice and other issues of human rights and responsibilities.

85. In both our Communions marriage has a God-given pattern and significance, entailing the life-long exclusive commitment of a man and a woman, encompassing the reciprocal love of husband and wife and the procreation and raising of children. Both Communions speak of marriage as a covenant and a vocation to holiness and see it in the order of creation as both sign and reality of God's faithful love.[157] It thus has a naturally sacramental dimension. "When God calls women and men to the married estate, and supports them in it, God's love for them is creative, redemptive and sanctifying."[158] In both Communions, the husband and wife are the celebrants of the sacrament. A priest normally has a special role in witnessing to the sacramental character of marriage.

86. Despite our common moral foundations, serious disagreements on specific issues exist, some of which have emerged in the long period of our separation:

a. Anglicans and Catholics have a different practice in respect of private confession. "The Reformers' emphasis on the direct access of the sinner to the forgiving and sustaining Word of God led Anglicans to reject the view that private confession before a priest was obligatory, although they continued to maintain that it was a wholesome means of grace, and made provision for it in the Book of Common Prayer for those with an unquiet and sorely troubled conscience."[159] Anglicans express this discipline

---

156 Cf. Lambeth Conference, 1930, Resolution 25 (reaffirmed at succeeding Lambeth Conferences) and also *Gaudium et Spes*, nn.77, 82.
157 Cf. Pope John Paul II's Apostolic Exhortation on the family, *Familiaris Consortio* (1981), n.34.
158 *Life in Christ*, n.60 (citing Lambeth Conference, 1968, Resolution 22).
159 *Life in Christ*, n.46.

in the short formula 'all may, none must, some should'. "The Roman Catholic Church, on the other hand, has continued to emphasise the sacrament of penance and the obligation, for those conscious of serious sin, of confessing their sins privately before a priest . . . (T)he discipline of the confession of sins before a priest has provided an important means of communicating the church's moral teaching and nurturing the spiritual lives of penitents."[160]

b. Whilst both Communions recognise that marriage is for life, both have also had to recognise the failure of many marriages in reality. For Roman Catholics, it is not possible however to dissolve the marriage bond once sacramentally constituted because of its indissoluble character, as it signifies the covenantal relationship of Christ with the Church. On certain grounds, however, the Catholic Church recognises that a true marriage was never contracted and a declaration of nullity may be granted by the proper authorities. Anglicans have been willing to recognise divorce following the breakdown of a marriage, and in recent years, some Anglican Churches have set forth circumstances in which they are prepared to allow partners from an earlier marriage to enter into another marriage.

c. Anglicans and Roman Catholics share the same fundamental teaching concerning the mystery of human life and the sanctity of the human person, but they differ in the way in which they develop and apply this fundamental moral teaching.[161] Anglicans have no agreed teaching concerning the precise moment from which the new human life developing in the womb is to be given the full protection due to a human person; not all Anglicans insist that in all circumstances, and without exception, such protection must extend back to conception. Among Anglicans the view is to be found that in certain cases direct abortion is morally justifiable.[162] Roman Catholic teaching is that the

---

160   *Ibid.* n.47.
161   *Ibid.* nn.85–86.
162   Lambeth Conference, 1930, Resolution 16 and Lambeth Conference, 1978, Resolution 10.

human embryo must be treated as a human person from the moment of conception and rejects all direct abortion.[163] Anglicans and Roman Catholics share an abhorrence of the growing practice in many countries of abortion on the grounds of mere convenience.

d. Anglicans and Roman Catholics agree that procreation is one of the divinely intended goods of the institution of marriage, and that a deliberate decision, without justifiable reason, to exclude procreation from marriage is a rejection of this good and a contradiction of the nature of marriage and how God calls couples to responsible parenthood. They agree that there are situations when a couple would be morally justified in avoiding bringing children into being.[164] They are not agreed on the method by which the responsibility of parents is exercised.[165] Catholic teaching requires that every act of intercourse should be open to procreation and counsels abstinence for couples who have a justifiable reason to avoid conception.[166] The Lambeth Conference in 1930 resolved that "where there is a morally sound reason for avoiding parenthood . . . and a sound reason for avoiding abstinence . . . other methods may be used."[167]

e. Anglicans and Roman Catholics affirm the importance of human friendship and affection among men and women, whether married or single, and believe, on the basis of scriptural teaching, that a faithful and life-long marriage provides the normative context for the expression of a fully sexual relationship. They reject the belief that married and homosexual relationships are morally equivalent.[168] Catholic teaching holds that homosexual activity is intrinsically disordered and always objectively wrong.[169] Strong tensions have surfaced within the

---

163 *Donum Vitae*, Pastoral Instruction of the Congregation of the Faith, 1987.
164 *Life in Christ*, n.78.
165 *Ibid.* nn.80–82.
166 *Humanae Vitae*, Encyclical Letter of Pope Paul VI (1968), n.11.
167 Lambeth Conference, 1930, Resolution 15 and Lambeth Conference, 1968, Resolution 22.
168 *Life in Christ*, n.87.
169 *Catechism of the Catholic Church* (1992), n.2357.

Anglican Communion because of serious challenges from within some Provinces[170] to the traditional teaching on human sexuality which was expressed in Resolution 1.10 of the 1998 Lambeth Conference.[171] Some Anglican diocesan and provincial synods have recently advocated the recognition and blessing of certain committed same-sex relationships within the life of the Church or within the life of civil society. The instruments of Communion have reaffirmed the Lambeth Resolution as the Anglican standard of teaching. In the discussions on human sexuality within the Anglican Communion, and between it and the Catholic Church, stand anthropological and biblical hermeneutical questions which need to be addressed.

87. We agree that there is a danger that areas of disagreement between us could expand as new issues and new contexts rapidly emerge. We need to study together and develop common structures for decision making in order to respond together to the issues already facing both our Churches and to new issues as they arise. We agree that we must act together, wherever possible, to prevent the integrity of Christian witness in the world from being further compromised. It is a matter of urgency that we take counsel, decide together, and act together in moral teaching, in order to guide and assist Christ's disciples in the way of holiness and to witness credibly and effectively to God's love and justice to the world.

9. The Blessed Virgin Mary

88. All generations of Anglicans and Roman Catholics have called the Virgin Mary 'blessed'. Anglicans and Roman Catholics agree

---

170   Namely, the election of a bishop in a same-sex relationship in the Episcopal Church (USA) and the authorisation of a public Rite of Blessing for same-sex unions in the Diocese of New Westminster in the Anglican Church of Canada.
171   Resolution 1.10 noted that "in view of the teaching of Scripture", the Conference "upholds faithfulness in marriage between a man and a woman in lifelong union, and believes that abstinence is right for those who are not called to marriage".

that it is impossible to be faithful to Scripture without giving due attention to the person of Mary.[172] Even though pieties and forms of teaching have developed independently in centuries of separation, it is still possible for us to express extensive agreement, based on the Scriptures and the ancient common traditions, on the place of Mary in the economy of salvation and the life of the Church. Within the contemporary life of our Communions we can discern much in common in our belief about the one who, of all believers, is closest to our Lord and Saviour Jesus Christ.

89. Anglicans and Catholics agree that there can be but one mediator between God and humanity, Jesus Christ, and reject any interpretation of the role of Mary which obscures this affirmation. We agree in recognising that Christian understanding of Mary is inseparably linked with the doctrines of Christ and of the Church. Catholics and Anglicans recognise the grace and unique vocation of Mary, Mother of God Incarnate (*Theotókos*), observe her festivals, and accord her honour in the communion of saints.[173] We learn that Mary was prepared by divine grace to be the mother of our Redeemer in accord with the biblical pattern of grace and hope. In view of this vocation to be the mother of the Holy One, it is fitting that Christ's redeeming work reached 'back' in Mary to the depths of her being and to her earliest beginnings.[174] It is also fitting to believe that the teaching that God has taken the Blessed Virgin Mary in the fullness of her person into his glory is consonant with Scripture, only to be understood in the light of Scripture, and is a sign of the eschatological hope of all humanity.[175] We agree in recognising in Mary a model of holiness, obedience and faith for all Christians and for the Church.[176]

---

172   *Mary: Grace and Hope in Christ*, n.6.
173   *Authority in the Church II*, n.30; *Mary: Grace and Hope in Christ*, n.2.
174   *Mary: Grace and Hope in Christ*, nn.54–55, 59.
175   *Ibid.* nn.56–58.
176   *Authority in the Church II*, n.30; *Mary: Grace and Hope in Christ*, n.2.

90. Anglicans and Roman Catholics share the ancient tradition of praying with and praising Mary. In the past, when Anglicans feared that devotional practices were presenting Mary as a mediator *in place of* Christ, direct invocation of Mary was avoided. Where no such danger is apparent, the practice of asking Mary, paramount in the Communion of Saints, to pray for us, has revived in some quarters. Catholics and Anglicans can acknowledge together that Mary has a continuing role in pointing Christians to Christ, the unique mediator; and that Mary and the saints pray for the whole Church. The practice of asking Mary and the saints to pray for us is not communion-dividing.[177] We are agreed that a range of pieties can be accommodated within our traditions when there is agreement in doctrine.

91. Through dialogue Anglicans and Roman Catholics have deepened their common understanding of Mary in the plan of salvation and the life of the Church. It is precisely because the Catholic Church saw the pattern of divine grace at work in Mary from the point of her conception through to her being received in glory that it came to define the Immaculate Conception and the Assumption as dogmas. It remains to be seen how, in the context of a visibly united Church, these doctrines would be affirmed in the confession of a common faith.

92. The practice of devotion to Mary and the invocation of the saints is a normal part of Catholic devotional life, but it remains for many Anglicans unfamiliar, or even alien. Further dialogue and mutual understanding is needed.

---

177 *Mary: Grace and Hope in Christ*, nn.64–75.

The faith that sets us free

93. The Commission gratefully acknowledges that the faith we hold in common is given to us by God. In this statement we have attempted to harvest the fruits of forty years of dialogue between Anglicans and Roman Catholics. As we reviewed the experience of our Churches it became clear to us how increased interaction has led to greater mutual understanding, and at the same time how this greater awareness of the extent of our shared faith has set us free to witness together more effectively. We celebrate and praise God for this.

94. There have been failures on the way and opportunities missed. We recognise that the obstacles that prevent us from receiving together all that God offers damage the effectiveness of our mission to the world. The Commission has become more profoundly aware of how intimately connected are understanding and cooperation, faith and mission. It is our conviction that, as we grow towards full, ecclesial communion and respond afresh to the common mission entrusted to his Church by our Lord, the remaining Church-dividing issues will be resolved more effectively.

95. Because we hope in the bountiful grace of God, we are encouraged to persevere, and to face the difficulties of growing together. We give glory to God, "whose power, working in us, can do infinitely more than we can ask or imagine; glory be to him from generation to generation in the Church and in Christ Jesus for ever and ever. Amen" (Ephesians 3.20–21).

Part Two

Towards Unity and
Common Mission

96. Genuine faith is more than assent: it is expressed in action. As Anglicans and Roman Catholics seek to overcome the remaining obstacles to full visible unity, we, the bishops of IARCCUM, recognise that the extent of common faith described in this statement compels us to live and witness together more fully here and now. Agreement in faith must go beyond mere affirmation. Discerning a common faith challenges our churches to recognise that elements of sanctification and truth exist in each other's ecclesial lives, and to develop those channels and practical expressions of co-operation by which a common life and mission may be generated and sustained.

97. We believe in a God whose life is communion and pure love, and that we ourselves share God's life in Christ through the Holy Spirit. All that we do as Anglicans and Roman Catholics, and, in particular, all that we seek to do together, should therefore be done in communion, with grace and generosity so that we do not obstruct the proclamation of the Good News. It is the call to generosity that is leading us now to share our gifts and our lives with one another, and it is the same call to generosity that prompts us to share with all people what God has given to us. The Church's mission flows intrinsically from our participation in the life of the one true God. We should always be seeking to share with one another and with the world at large the good gifts of the living God.

98. We also recognise the progress which has been made in our relations with other Christians and remain committed to the reconciliation of all Christian people. Wherever Anglicans and Roman Catholics take steps to deepen our relationship with one another in life and mission, we should be sensitive to our other ecumenical partnerships, acting in ways consistent with agreements we have already entered into.

99. We, the bishops of IARCCUM, invite Anglicans and Roman Catholics everywhere to consider the following suggestions. They are offered as practical examples of the kind of joint action in mission that we believe our shared faith now invites us to pursue and which would deepen the communion we share. We also recognise, however, that the context and dynamics of relationships between Anglicans and Roman Catholics differ widely across the

world. There may be compelling reasons why some of the suggestions and invitations set out below are neither appropriate nor feasible in some local contexts. Nevertheless the fruits of the dialogue between Anglicans and Catholics over forty years constitute an exhortation for all Anglicans and Catholics to consider how we may carry forward our commitment to full visible unity, and we commend the ideas and proposals set out below for careful consideration and reflection.

1. Visible expressions of our shared faith

Both the Roman Catholic Church and the Churches of the Anglican Communion are liturgical Churches in which God is glorified in common public worship. We invite Anglicans and Roman Catholics to develop strategies to foster the visible expression of their shared faith.

100. Given our mutual recognition of one another's baptism, a number of practical initiatives are possible. Local churches may consider developing joint programmes for the formation of families when they present children for baptism, as well as preparing common catechetical resources for use in baptismal and confirmation preparation and in Sunday Schools. We suggest that our local parishes regularly make a public profession of faith together, perhaps by renewing baptismal promises at Pentecost each year. We invite local churches to use the same baptismal certificate, and, where necessary, to review and improve those currently in use. While respecting current canonical requirements, we also encourage the inclusion of witnesses from the other church at baptisms and confirmations, particularly in the case of candidates from interchurch families. We encourage co-operation in faith renewal programmes which aim to help reclaim the baptismal commitment of people in the course of their adult life.

101. Given the significant extent of our common understanding of the Eucharist (cf. paragraphs 39 to 44 above), and the central importance of the Eucharist to our faith, we encourage attendance at each other's Eucharists, respecting the different disciplines of our churches.[178] This is particularly appropriate during the Week

---

178 Discipline in the Catholic Church is set out in the *Ecumenical Directory*, nn.129–32; Anglican discipline varies from province to province.

of Prayer for Christian Unity and other festive occasions in the life of our local communities. This would provide opportunities for experiencing each other's eucharistic life, thereby serving both to deepen our communion and our desire for full communion. While this would take the form of non-communicating attendance in each other's churches, it would nonetheless initiate a renewed awareness of the value of spiritual communion. We commend the offering of a blessing which has become a regular practice in some places for those who may not receive holy communion.

102. We also encourage more frequent joint non-eucharistic worship, including celebrations of faith, pilgrimages, processions of witness (e.g. on Good Friday), and shared public liturgies on significant occasions. We encourage those who pray the daily office to explore how celebrating daily prayer together can reinforce their common mission.

103. We encourage Anglicans and Roman Catholics to pray for the local bishop of the other church as well as for their own bishop, and for God's blessing on their co-operation where possible in their leadership of the local churches' mission. We welcome the growing Anglican custom of including in the prayers of the faithful a prayer for the Pope, and we invite Roman Catholics to pray regularly in public for the Archbishop of Canterbury and the leaders of the Anglican Communion.

2. Joint study of our faith

Given the degree of agreement in faith outlined in this statement, we wish to promote joint study in order to deepen the faith we share.

104. Since the Scriptures hold a prime place in the life of faith for both Anglicans and Catholics, we encourage joint study of the Scriptures, particularly by those in training for ministry. Ecumenical translations of the Bible are invaluable resources in our efforts to engage in common witness. We note the close similarities of Anglican and Roman Catholic lectionaries which make it possible to foster joint bible study groups based upon the Sunday lectionary. We also encourage the development of common

hermeneutical principles (see paragraphs 26 to 30 above) in order to reach an agreed ecumenical reading of the Scriptures. This could be nurtured through shared sponsorship of lectures and workshops on different methodological approaches, both ancient and modern, to the Scriptures. Lastly, we suggest the introduction of joint workshops for preachers, as well as shared study of each other's liturgical traditions.

105. In reflecting on our faith together it is vital that all bishops ensure that the Agreed Statements of ARCIC are widely studied in both Communions. In addition to ARCIC I's *Final Report* (1982), we invite joint study of the work of the second phase of ARCIC. For instance, *Church as Communion* reflects on the mystery of the Church and the visible elements of communion necessary for full visible unity, which can help Anglicans and Roman Catholics to identify the constitutive elements of the Church in each other's life and witness and, as they discern elements in common, can assist them to consider how they may come together in their living of them. A study of *Life in Christ: Morals, Communion and the Church* could deepen mutual understanding of our shared moral principles as well as our remaining differences. We encourage the setting up of discussion groups on the recent Agreed Statement, *Mary: Grace and Hope in Christ,* with a view to gaining a greater appreciation of our common Mariological heritage and to reflecting upon the practical implications of the Commission's findings.[179]

106. National or regional Anglican – Roman Catholic Commissions (ARCs) already exist in several parts of the world, and they have made significant contributions through engaging in theological dialogue and discerning various avenues for pastoral co-operation (e.g. in the Caribbean, USA, England and Wales, Canada, Australia, New Zealand). Anglican provinces and Catholic episcopal conferences might consider the establishment of ARCs where they

---

179   Cf. Timothy Bradshaw, *Commentary and Study Guide on the Seattle Statement of the Anglican – Roman Catholic International Commission, Mary: Grace and Hope in Christ* (London: Anglican Communion Office, 2005); *Mary: Grace and Hope in Christ – The Text with Commentaries and Study Guide,* ed. Donald Bolen and Gregory Cameron (London: Continuum, 2006).

do not exist. In addition to their local impact, they also can have a valuable role in assisting the reception of the Agreed Statements of ARCIC and in offering information to the International Commission about the development of relationships at the local level.

107. There are numerous theological resources that can be shared, including professional staff, libraries, and formation and study programmes for clergy and laity. The possibilities for sharing that are already open to us, e.g. those identified in *The Ecumenical Dimension in the Formation of those Engaged in Pastoral Work*,[180] should be explored and implemented to their fullest potential.

3. Co-operation in ministry

We encourage co-operation wherever possible in lay and ordained ministries.

108. In addition to national ARCs, regional Anglican – Roman Catholic bishops' dialogues have also been established in various places with a view to addressing pastoral issues and creating a context in which trust and friendship develop in the mutual love of Christ. This type of dialogue has proved fruitful, for example, in providing guidelines for interchurch families and other social and pastoral situations. Where such dialogue does not already take place, we encourage Anglican and Roman Catholic bishops to consider the value of annual or more frequent meetings.[181]

109. Striving towards unity involves the resolution of divisive issues from the past, but it also requires close communication so as to address ongoing developments within our respective Communions. Wherever possible, ordained and lay observers can be invited to attend each other's synodical and collegial gatherings and conferences. We also encourage Anglican and Roman Catholic leaders, on both the international and national levels, to consult one another as fully as possible before crucial decisions touching the unity of the Church are taken in matters of faith, order, or moral life.

---

180   *The Ecumenical Dimension in the Formation of those Engaged in Pastoral Work* (Vatican City: Vatican Press, 1997).
181   For instance, Anglican and Roman Catholic bishops in the Sudan have met regularly over the past four years and have effectively and jointly addressed important social themes.

110. We encourage bishops to undertake joint study of recent Roman Catholic and Anglican documents[182] so as to enable common teaching on matters pertaining to local mission and witness. There is an obvious value when Church leaders issue joint pastoral statements on urgent matters of common concern at regional and national levels and we urge all bishops to do so whenever possible.

111. Beyond these forms of consultation, a range of other initiatives at the episcopal level could be envisaged. We see a particular value in the practice of providing letters of introduction to ecumenical colleagues whenever a new bishop is elected. Consideration could be given to the association of Anglican bishops with Roman Catholic bishops in their *ad limina* visits to Rome.[183] Episcopal consultation and co-operation in the formulation of protocols for handling the movement of clergy from one Communion to the other is encouraged.

112. Given the extent of our common understanding of ministry, we encourage exploring possibilities for engaging in some aspects of joint formation. Jointly sponsored workshops for newly ordained bishops could highlight ways in which their ministry could be attentive to ecumenical concerns, for instance, by fostering the sort of consultation and pastoral co-operation outlined above. In preparation for priestly ministry, while bearing in mind distinct elements of formation, thought can be given to appropriate co-operation in theological education (e.g. in the fields of biblical studies, church history, pastoral formation). There is a possibility for even more extensive co-operation in the fields of diaconal training and ongoing clergy formation, including joint clergy retreats.

113. While not losing sight of underlying doctrinal problems regarding the mutual recognition of orders (cf. paragraphs 60 to 61 above), every appropriate opportunity can be taken to acknowledge

---

182   In the Catholic Church this would include texts such as papal encyclicals and other authoritative teachings. In the Anglican Communion this would include reports of Commissions of the Anglican Communion, material from the four Instruments of Communion, and other study papers.
183   We note that this has already occurred in the case of a recent *ad limina* visit of Roman Catholic bishops from Papua New Guinea.

publicly the fruitfulness of each other's ordained ministries, for example by attending each other's ordinations.

114. We urge Anglicans and Roman Catholics to explore together how the ministry of the Bishop of Rome might be offered and received in order to assist our Communions to grow towards full, ecclesial communion.[184]

115. Anglicans and Roman Catholics share a rich heritage regarding the place of religious orders in ecclesial life. There are religious communities in both of our Communions that trace their origins to the same founders (e.g. Benedictines and Franciscans). We encourage the continuation and strengthening of relations between Anglican and Catholic religious orders, and acknowledge the particular witness of monastic communities with an ecumenical vocation.

116. There are many areas where pastoral and spiritual care can be shared. We acknowledge the benefit derived from many instances of spiritual direction given and received by Anglicans to Catholics and Catholics to Anglicans. Of particular concern in the area of ministry is the need to develop programmes of joint pastoral care for interchurch families (including marriage preparation) and to find ways to minister to their concerns.

117. We recommend joint training where possible for lay ministries (e.g. catechists, lectors, readers, teachers, evangelists). We commend the sharing of the talents and resources of lay ministers, particularly between local Anglican and Roman Catholic parishes. We note the potential for music ministries to enrich our relations and to strengthen the Church's outreach to the wider society, especially young people.

4. Shared witness in the world

We encourage fostering a mission-orientated spirituality of engagement with the world and developing joint strategies of outreach so as to share our faith.

118. We recognise the intimate relationship between the unity of the Church, the peace and well-being of the human community, and

---

184   Cf. *Ut Unum Sint*, n.96. *The Gift of Authority*, n.59.

the integrity of all creation. We urge our two Communions to work together globally with others to promote social justice, to eradicate poverty and to care for the environment (e.g. by supporting the Millennium Development Goals set out by the United Nations).

119. We also encourage local churches to join together in making contributions to public life, giving voice to Christian perspectives on important social questions. We urge Anglicans and Roman Catholics in their social witness to act upon the principle that we should do all things together excepting only those things that deep differences compel us to do separately (cf. the Lund Principle), particularly given the agreement in faith we have set out in this Statement.

120. Wherever we as churches have been guilty of contributing to tensions and strife of a political, socio-economic or religious nature, we should demonstrate a willingness to repent of our actions and to move toward reconciliation.[185] In so doing we hope that we might be able to give witness before the wider society to the necessity of ongoing conversion and to Christian processes of conflict resolution. In many instances, such witness will express itself by co-operation with governments or secular bodies which seek to bring reconciliation to their communities.[186]

121. We encourage joint participation in evangelism, developing specific strategies to engage with those who have yet to hear and respond to the Gospel. We invite churches to study together the biblical foundations for evangelism as they apply to the local cultural context of mission. We recognise the importance of the shared training of lay people for evangelism, and the development of new ways of gathering faith communities.

122. We invite our churches to consider the development of joint Anglican/Roman Catholic church schools, shared teacher training programmes and contemporary religious education curricula for use in our schools. We are conscious of the pressing need for new

---

185 E.g. Pope John Paul II's initiatives at the close of the last millennium to promote repentance for the Church's past failings.
186 E.g. The Truth and Reconciliation Commission in South Africa.

57

ways to reach youth, and believe that young people would themselves welcome creative joint outreach programmes.

123. While continuing to strengthen Anglican – Roman Catholic relations both through theological dialogue and common mission, we remain committed to the wider unity of all Christians. In order to safeguard the cohesion of our engagement in the ecumenical movement and to extend the parameters of agreements in faith which we have reached, we strongly encourage close consultation when one of us engages in a new ecumenical partnership with another church, whether locally, regionally or at a world level.

124. Local churches could learn from the contribution to the Church's mission made by new groups, movements and associations within our Communions, particularly those movements whose charism includes a strong commitment to Christian unity.

125. We recommend working more closely together in our relations with adherents of other religions. We are particularly mindful of the value of speaking with a common voice as Christians amidst situations of conflict, misunderstanding and mistrust, especially when Christians or those of other faith communities live as vulnerable minorities.

Conclusion

126. We the bishops of IARCCUM strongly commend these suggestions to members of the episcopate around the world, mindful of the specific responsibilities of bishops for the promotion of Christian unity and the mission of the Church. We give thanks to God for the extensive theological consensus articulated in this document – fruits of the last forty years of dialogue – and we pray that God will richly bless all that we are now called to do in His Name. We call on all bishops to encourage their clergy and people to respond positively to this initiative, and to engage in a searching exploration of new possibilities for co-operation in mission.

Appendix 1: Unity and Mission

A. Roman Catholic Perspectives

127. The bishops gathered at the Second Vatican Council, in their Decree on Ecumenism, *Unitatis Redintegratio*, stated that "promoting the restoration of unity" was one of their "chief concerns". They declared that "The Church, established by Christ the Lord is, indeed, one and unique", and that the discord between different Christian communions "openly contradicts the will of Christ, provides a stumbling block to the world and inflicts damage on the most holy cause of proclaiming the good news to every creature".[187] These convictions concerning ecumenism and mission have been further developed in the encyclical letters *Redemptoris Missio* (1987) and *Ut Unum Sint* (1995).

128. In addition to noting the damage caused to God's mission by disunity, Pope John Paul II, in his encyclical *Redemptoris Missio*, underlined the positive opportunities that our common baptism in Christ opens up. He emphasised the need for collaboration in a spirit of fellowship with "separated brothers and sisters", in accordance with the norms of *Unitatis Redintegratio*. This imperative is to be carried out "by a common profession of faith in God and in Jesus Christ before the nations – to the extent that this is possible – and by their co-operation in social and technical as well as in cultural and religious matters."[188] The scope for common profession and co-operation has subsequently been translated into practical principles and norms in the *Ecumenical Directory* produced by the Pontifical Council for Promoting Christian Unity. A wide range of options is set out, including ecumenical co-operation in mission engagement with the "de-Christianised masses of our contemporary world", in a way that avoids unhealthy rivalry and sectarianism.[189] The principles and norms also encompass interfaith dialogue and the fields of development, human need, healthcare and the stewardship of creation.

B. Anglican Perspectives

129. The Anglican Communion's entry into the ecumenical movement was grounded in its commitment to mission. Following the Edinburgh

---

187   *Unitatis Redintegratio*, n.1.
188   *Redemptoris Missio*. n.50.
189   *Ecumenical Directory*, n.208.

Missionary Conference in 1910, the 1920 Lambeth Conference issued an "Appeal to all Christian People" in which the bishops asked "that all should unite in a new and great endeavour to recover and to manifest to the world the unity of the body of Christ for which he prayed".[190] The bishops affirmed "we believe that it is God's purpose to manifest this fellowship, so far as the world is concerned, in an outward, visible, and united society . . . using God given means of grace, and inspiring all members to the world wide service of the kingdom of God". It is this vocation to the world for which Christ gave his life out of divine love that has energised the effort towards Christian unity.

130. Our mission relationships as Anglicans must be seen as part of the wider mission relationships of all Christians. The experience of the last years of the 20th century underlined the importance of the Lambeth call for Anglicans to explore ways of being involved in mission co-operatively with other Christians. We need the stimulation, the critique and the encouragement of sisters and brothers in Christ of other traditions. A constant question before us must be, to what extent are we faithful in inviting those of other traditions to participate in advising and working with us in our outreach?

131. Building on this foundational commitment, as a result of great strides in theological consensus, the bishops at the 1998 Lambeth Conference reaffirmed the longstanding Anglican commitment to the full visible unity of the Church as the goal of the ecumenical movement.[191] Visible unity of the Church is "to point to the sort of life God intends for the whole of humanity, a foretaste of God's Kingdom". They describe what they call "a portrait of visible unity" emerging in ecumenical conversations. Visible unity "entails agreement in faith together with the common celebration of the sacraments, supported by a united ministry and forms of collegial and conciliar consultation in matters of faith, life and witness . . . For the fullness of communion all these visible aspects of the life of the Church require to be permeated by a profound spiritual communion, a growing together in a common mind, mutual concern and a care for unity (Philippians 2.2)."[192] The Lambeth Conference stressed that visible unity entails a rich diversity which is the necessary result of the Gospel being lived out in specific cultural and particular historical contexts.

---

190   Section IX of Resolution 9.
191   Resolution IV.1.
192   'Called to be One: Section IV Report', in *The Official Report of the Lambeth Conference 1998*, citing *The Porvoo Common Statement* (London: Council for Christian Unity of the General Synod of the Church of England, 1993), n.28.

Anglican and Roman Catholic Joint Commitment to Unity and Mission

132. Following Vatican II, Pope Paul VI and Archbishop Michael Ramsey in their Common Declaration, 1966, spoke of their intention to inaugurate a serious dialogue which might lead to "that unity in truth for which Christ prayed". They spoke of "a restoration of complete communion of faith and sacramental life". They declared that they were "of one mind in their determination . . . to strive in common to find solutions for all the great problems that face the Church in the world of today".[193] In 1977 Pope Paul VI and Archbishop Donald Coggan spoke of this goal as "Christ's will",[194] and said that progress to unity will include a consideration of Christ's intentions in founding the Church. "Communion with God in Christ through faith and through baptism and self-giving to Him . . . stands at the centre of our witness to the world, even while between us communion remains imperfect."[195] They went on to declare, "our divisions hinder this witness, hinder the work of Christ but they do not close all roads we may travel together. In a spirit of prayer and submission to God's will we must collaborate more earnestly in a greater common witness to Christ before the world in the very work of evangelisation".[196] In 1989, Pope John Paul II and Archbishop Robert Runcie reaffirmed this understanding of Christ's will for the Church in their joint declaration: "Christian unity is demanded so that the Church can be a more effective sign of God's kingdom of love and justice for all humanity."[197] In 1996, Pope John Paul II and Archbishop George Carey stressed that, "whenever [Anglicans and Catholics] are able to give united witness to the Gospel they must do so, for our divisions obscure the Gospel message of reconciliation and hope."[198]

133. ARCIC in its agreed statement *Church as Communion* includes a detailed description of the visible unity that Anglicans and Roman Catholics seek together. The constitutive elements of ecclesial communion include: one faith, one baptism, the one Eucharist, acceptance of basic moral values, a

---

193 The Common Declaration by Pope Paul VI and the Archbishop of Canterbury Dr Michael Ramsey, March 24, 1966, in ARCIC I's *The Final Report*, pp. 117–18.

194 The Common Declaration by Pope Paul VI and the Archbishop of Canterbury Dr Donald Coggan, April 29,1977, in *The Final Report*, pp. 119–122, here citing n.7, p. 121.

195 *Ibid.* n.9, p. 121.

196 *Ibid.*

197 The Common Declaration by Pope John Paul II and the Archbishop of Canterbury Dr Robert Runcie, October 2, 1989, in *Information Service* 71 (1989/III-IV), pp. 122–23.

198 The Common Declaration by Pope John Paul II and the Archbishop of Canterbury Dr George Carey, December 5, 1996, in *Information Service* 94 (1997/I), pp. 20–21.

ministry of oversight entrusted to the episcopate with collegial and primatial dimensions, and the episcopal ministry of a universal primate as the visible focus of unity.[199] The report acknowledges that the theme of communion as a description of the nature of the Church "confronts Christians with the scandal of our divisions" since "Christian disunity obscures God's invitation to communion for all humankind and makes the Gospel we proclaim harder to hear".[200]

134. While Anglicans and Roman Catholics in common declarations of Popes and Archbishops of Canterbury and in their bilateral dialogue have stressed the goal of visible unity and the urgency of working together towards that goal for the sake of the Church's mission, this calling has always been understood within the goal of visible unity of all Christians. When Pope John Paul II and Archbishop Robert Runcie set up the second phase of ARCIC they said that the aim was "not limited to the union of our two Communions alone, to the exclusion of other Christians, but rather [it] extends to the fulfilment of God's will for the visible unity of all his people".[201] Furthermore, both Pope John Paul II in his encyclical *Ut Unum Sint* and the bishops at the Lambeth Conference in 1998 refer to the goal of unity set out in the statement of the Canberra Assembly of the World Council of Churches, *The Unity of the Church as* Koinonia: *Gift and Calling*.[202]

135. The Anglican and Roman Catholic bishops at their Mississauga meeting in May 2000 came together to consider the journey towards visible unity and the imperative of unity if the Church is to fulfil its role of healing and reconciling a broken and divided world. They stated, "We have come to a clear sense that we have moved much closer to the goal of full visible communion than we had at first dared to believe. A sense of mutual interdependence in the Body of Christ has been reached, in which the churches of the Anglican Communion and the Roman Catholic Church are able to bring shared gifts to their joint mission in the world".[203] As identified in the Introduction to the present document (paragraphs 6 to 10 above), intervening events have raised challenges to the goals set at Mississauga. In asking how we are to be faithful amidst present complexities to the vision which has propelled our dialogue these past decades, we reiterate that even in a time of uncertainty, the mission given us by Christ in the power of the Holy Spirit ever calls us to give tangible expression to the degree of faith we share through common mission, joint witness and shared prayer.

199 *Church as Communion*, n.43.

200 *Ibid.* n.4.

201 The Common Declaration by Pope John Paul II and the Archbishop of Canterbury Dr Robert Runcie, May 29, 1982, in *Information Service* 49 (1989/II-III), pp. 46–47, here citing n.5, p. 47.

202 *Ut Unum Sint*, n.78; Lambeth Conference 1998, Resolution IV.7e and Resolution IV.24a; 'The Canberra Statement' (*op. cit.*).

203 *Communion in Mission*, n.6.

Appendix 2: The documents of ARCIC

FIRST PHASE
1971 'Eucharistic Doctrine'
1973 'Ministry and Ordination'
1976 'Authority in the Church I'
1979 Elucidation of 'Eucharistic Doctrine'
1979 Elucidation of 'Ministry'
1981 Elucidation of 'Authority in the Church I'
1981 'Authority in the Church II'
In 1982, these documents were published together with a preface,
    introduction and conclusion, as *The Final Report.*

SECOND PHASE
1987 'Salvation and the Church'
1991 'Church as Communion'
1994 'Life in Christ: Morals, Communion and the Church'
1999 'The Gift of Authority: Authority in the Church III'
2005 'Mary: Grace and Hope in Christ'

Appendix 3: The membership of IARCCUM

Anglicans

Bishop David Beetge, Church of the Province of Southern Africa, Co-
    Chairman
Archbishop Peter Carnley, Anglican Church of Australia
Bishop Peter Fox, Anglican Church of Papua New Guinea, 2005
Bishop Edwin Gulick, Episcopal Church USA
Archbishop Peter Kwong, Hong Kong Sheng Kung Hui, 2001–2004
Bishop Michael Nazir-Ali, Church of England
The Revd Canon Jonathan Gough, Archbishop of Canterbury's
    representative, 2001–2004
The Revd Canon Andrew Norman, Archbishop of Canterbury's
    representative, 2005
    Dr Mary Tanner, Church of England
The Revd Canon Gregory Cameron, Anglican Communion Office, Co-
    Secretary from 2003

Consultants
Bishop John Baycroft, Anglican Church of Canada, from 2003 (Co-Secretary 2002)
Bishop David Hamid, Gibraltar in Europe, from 2002 (Co-Secretary 2001)

Roman Catholics

Archbishop John Bathersby, Australia, Co-Chairman
Archbishop Alexander Brunett, USA
Bishop Anthony Farquhar, Ireland
Bishop Crispian Hollis, England
Bishop Lucius Ugorji, Nigeria
The Revd Dr Peter Cross, Australia (deceased 2006)
Sr Dr Donna Geernaert, Canada
The Revd Donald Bolen, Pontifical Council for Promoting Christian Unity, Co-Secretary

Consultants
Monsignor Timothy Galligan, England, from 2002
The Revd Dr Paul McPartlan, from 2003

Administrative Staff

Mrs Christine Codner, Anglican Communion Office, 2001–2004
The Revd Terrie Robinson, Anglican Communion Office, 2005
Ms Giovanna Ramon, Pontifical Council for Promoting Christian Unity